CENTRAL NEW YORK BEER

A History of Brewing in the Heart of the Empire State

DANIEL SHUMWAY

AMERICAN PALATE

Published by American Palate
A Division of The History Press
Charleston, SC 29403
www.historypress.net

Cover image: Otsego Lake. *Courtesy of John Kocijanski of Catskills Photography.*

First published 2014

Manufactured in the United States

ISBN 978.1.62619.342.0

Library of Congress CIP data applied for.

CONTENTS

ACKNOWLEDGEMENTS

I would like to thank the curators at the Oneida County Historical Society, the curators at the Rome Historical Society and the curators at the Herkimer County Historical Society. They provided old city directories, maps and old newspapers on microfilm for me to review. I would also like to thank Ralph Van Norstrom from Norwich, New York, who provided information on the breweries of Norwich.

Thomas M. Tryniski deserves a big thank-you for creating the Fulton history website, which contains over 23.5 million New York State newspaper pages in pdf format and allows you to perform searches of the pages. This is a great help in finding information on old breweries and the people who ran them. When you don't know when events happened, this is a quick way to find out.

I would like to thank the members of the BCCA (Brewery Collectibles Club of America) and the ECBA (Eastern Coast Breweriana Association) whom I have met over the past forty years and who have instilled in me a love of brewing and brewery history.

Finally, I would like to thank my wife, Barb, who put up with my hobby. She attends shows and conventions with me and enjoys the hobby.

INTRODUCTION

This is the second book I have written about breweries in New York State. In my first book, I covered the history of breweries in Utica. In this book, I have covered all the breweries located within a fifty-mile radius of Utica from the early 1800s to present time. The eighteen cities/villages covered are Boonville, Canajoharie, Canastota, Cazenovia, Cooperstown, Fort Plain, Garrattsville, Hamilton, Herkimer, Ilion, Little Falls, Milford, Norwich, Oneonta, Oriskany Falls, Rome, Waterville and Westmoreland.

In the two-hundred-plus years covered in this book, these cities/villages have had over sixty-two breweries. The city of Rome had the most, with seventeen breweries. Cooperstown followed with seven. As of 2014, there are nine operating or soon-to-be-operating breweries in the fifty-mile radius around Utica. Of these breweries, five have started up recently.

In 2012, New York State passed a bill to allow small breweries called farm breweries to get tax breaks and other benefits. To get a farm brewery license, a brewery must make beer that contains at least 20 percent of New York State–grown products. By 2018, this usage will increase to 60 percent and must be 90 percent by 2024. The farm brewery license allows a brewery to open restaurants, increase tastings and sell related products. It also increases the number of retail outlets in which a brewery's products can be sold. This bill was modeled after a wine bill that has been in effect in New York State since the 1990s. Since the bill's passage, fourteen farm brewery licenses have been issued in 2014. Within the scope of this book, three breweries are operating as farm breweries: Good Nature Brewing in Hamilton, Erie Canal Brewing in Canastota and Henneberg Brewing in Cazenovia.

The new law promotes using local products and addresses the current popularity of craft-brewed beer. People are enjoying the many choices of beer and styles that are being made. New breweries are popping up all over the state, which is helping local economies. As the old saying goes, "This isn't your father's beer anymore!" Try all the new flavors, you are bound to find one you like.

Finding information on breweries that operated before 1850 is quite difficult. Newspapers and city directories are scarce and usually do not contain much information. While I have identified sixty-two breweries that operated in the region, there were probably more in the years before 1850. Many breweries from that time period were very small and usually run by people who had inns or taverns. The product they made was served only at their establishments and maybe to their neighbors.

The breweries contained in this book suffered from fires, robberies, a suicide and Prohibition. Very few survived these events to make comebacks. As travel became easier during the last half of the 1800s, breweries in the small villages and cities surrounding Utica started to fail. Larger brewers from Utica and other bigger cities from around the country were shipping their products to these villages and cities—and at a cheaper cost than could be offered by the local breweries. As a result, these small breweries began to fail. By the time Prohibition took effect, only three breweries remained in operation: Evans & Giehl in Rome, Norwich Brewing in Norwich and Bierbauer Brewing in Canajoharie. After Prohibition ended in 1933, only two breweries started back up under new names: the brewery in Rome, which lasted to 1942, and the brewery in Canajoharie, which only lasted until 1934.

During Prohibition, three places had wildcat (illegal) breweries operating within the village/city limits. In Rome, the old Amtmann brewery was used for one of the largest bootlegger operations in the area. It was discovered and shut down in 1927. Also in Rome, the old Evans & Giehl brewery, which was operating as the Rome Cereal Beverage Company, was shut down in 1926 for violations of the Volstead Act. Finally, the old Bierbauer brewery in Canajoharie was raided in 1922, when agents discovered a wildcat brewery operating on the premises.

The future of brewing in New York State appears to be bright. The craft-brewing phenomenon continues to expand, offering consumers a wide variety of beer styles. Tourism is growing in the villages and cities that contain these businesses, as many people enjoy visiting breweries. I have visited over fifty breweries a year for the last three years and plan to continue to visit as many as possible in the future. New York State has passed legislation that encourages small breweries to start up and has helped the state's existing brewers expand and prosper.

CHAPTER 1
BOONVILLE BREWERIES
1889–1891

B oonville is located to the north of Utica in Oneida County. The first settlers arrived from the Netherlands in 1795 and called the village *Kortenaer* after a Dutch admiral. The village was incorporated in 1855 and was renamed Boonville after Gerrit Boon, an agent of the Holland Land Company. The village had only one main brewery, which repeatedly burned down.

KILKENNY & KITTS BREWING COMPANY, 1889–90

In the spring of 1889, Charles Kilkenny and George B. Kitts decided to start a brewery in Boonville, New York. They felt that the area could support a small brewery. A site was chosen at the junction of the Black River Canal feeder and the canal itself in the northeastern part of the village known as "Coney Island." Citizens subscribed enough to purchase the site.

Charles Kilkenny was born in West Branch, Oneida County, on January 22, 1857. He ran a general store in Forestport for two years, at the age of nineteen. After that, he learned the trade of butcher and operated a meat market in Boonville for five years before deciding to get into the brewing business.

The partners purchased the land from Sarah G. Lee on July 8, 1889. The deed was recorded in the county clerk's office on July 21, 1889, along with all fixtures, tools, implements and apparatus contained in the brewery on the property.

The new brewery would produce only ale and had a capacity of three hundred barrels per week. The firm of Fardette Bros. of Boonville was hired to construct the new brewery. The brewery consisted of a large, two-story frame building that housed the brewing equipment and supplies. An attached stone building contained the engine and boiler used to power the brewery. The office was in a nearby building, and there were stables for the horses and delivery wagon. The brewery cost $7,500 to build. By June of that year, the brewery was complete. Brewing started in July and, when released to the public, was well received. The company did a brisk business that fall and winter as word spread about its product.

On June 25, 1890, the brewery was destroyed by fire. At about 2:30 a.m., a fire was discovered on the second story of the brewery. An alarm was given, and the fire department was quick to appear at the site. By then, however, the entire building had been engulfed in flames, and nothing could be done except to protect the surrounding buildings and the brewery office. The firemen worked feverishly until 5:00 a.m., when the fire was finally brought under control.

The fire destroyed the main building, all the brewing equipment and about two hundred barrels of stock ale. The engine and boiler escaped with only minor damage. The books and office safe were found intact. The loss was placed at $8,000, which was partially covered by insurance. The W.D. Sippell Agency of Boonville held the insurance policies for the brewery. The policies were written by several London firms and consisted of $4,000 on the building and machinery and $1,500 on the stock. The origin of the fire was unknown at the time but was later suspected to have been the result of arson. There was a large temperance movement in the area at this time, so it is quite likely that the fires were started by someone who thought drinking beer was evil. The brewery was rebuilt, but Kitts decided to get out of the business.

BOONVILLE BREWING COMPANY, 1890–1891

Shortly after the fire destroyed the Kilkenny & Kitts Brewing Company, Charles Kilkenny and several other investors decided to rebuild the brewery on the same site. The decision to rebuild was based largely on the brisk business that the old brewery had been doing.

On July 24, 1890, articles of incorporation for the Boonville Brewing Company were filed in the county clerk's office. Capital stock for the brewery

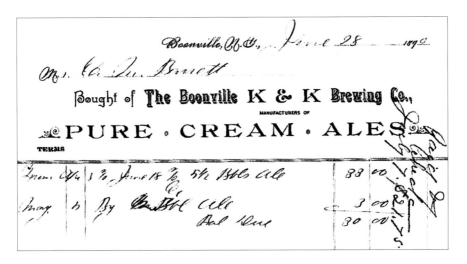

Boonville Kilkenny & Kitts Brewing Company letterhead from 1890. *Author's collection.*

was set at $10,000, to be divided into one hundred shares. The trustees for the first year were Charles Kilkenny, Frank A. Barrett, George M. Sawyer and Peter Phillips. The brewery would produce ale, beer and soda.

The new brewery was a three-story frame building that was slightly larger than the old one. The stone engine room and stables remained as they were. Construction was finished in September, and brewing commenced in October.

This was an ale brewery, like its predecessor. The ale that was produced was well liked by the local population, and the brewery became profitable very quickly.

On January 3, 1891, fire again struck the brewery. At 2:15 a.m., flames were discovered bursting from the windows of the main building. The fire had gained great headway before the alarm sounded and the fire department arrived on the scene. The air was very cold at the time, and there was a sharp north wind, which made it difficult for the firemen to keep up proper steam in the fire engine.

The firemen quickly realized that it would be useless to try to save the main structure and turned their attention to the adjoining stone building. The frame portion of the brewery burned to the ground, and the stone building was damaged severely.

The fire was believed to have been deliberately set. A fire had been discovered on the premises early on the morning of January 2 but was extinguished before gaining much headway. A watchman was then put on guard until midnight, after which the building was empty. The arsonist entered the building sometime after midnight to start the fire. The owners felt that the fire back in June and this one were set by the same person, probably a prohibitionist.

The estimated value of the building and stock was $10,000. The property was covered by $7,000 worth of insurance spread equally among the Westchester, German American, Guardian, Bowery and the Niagara & Phoenix of Brooklyn insurance companies. The arsonist was never caught and in the end got his way. The brewery was never rebuilt, even though it had been very profitable for the short time it operated. No other breweries were ever built in Boonville.

Charles Kilkenny died on June 14, 1922, from a heart attack while working in his office. He was sixty-five years old. After leaving the brewing business, Kilkenny became involved in the buying and selling of horses for racing for fifteen years. After that, he worked in Utica, where he dealt in real estate and made loans. He also was a deputy sheriff for several years. He was survived by his wife, Stella, and three brothers.

On April 1, 1924, the governor of New York declared that the Boonville Brewing Company was dissolved and its charter forfeited by reason of failure to report as required by the stock corporation law.

Chapter 2
CANAJOHARIE BREWERIES
1869–1934

Canajoharie is located forty-three miles to the east of Utica in Montgomery County. It was settled by Palatine German settlers and was originally called Roofville after early inhabitant Johannes Rueff. The village was incorporated in 1829. It was almost obliterated by three fires in the nineteenth century. The village was renamed Canajoharie at a later date, after the Mohawk Indian village of the same name. The name *Canajoharie* in Iroquois means "the pot that washes itself," which is a reference to a circular gorge in Canajoharie Creek, just south of the village. When built, the Erie Canal passed through the north side of the village.

Until recently, the village was the home of the Beech-Nut Baby Food Company. The plant closed in 2011 and moved to Florida, New York. Many famous people originated from here or were employed here. Susan B. Anthony, the women's rights pioneer, taught school in Canajoharie. Joseph Brant, the Mohawk chief, and Rebecca Winters, a Mormon pioneer, both resided here. The current population of the village is 2,230.

LOUIS BIERBAUER BREWERY, 1869–1904

Louis Bierbauer was born on March 20, 1832, in Barsrid, Germany. He came to this country in 1842 and lived in New York City. He moved to Canajoharie in 1860 and erected a brewery on Mill Street in 1869.

Drawing of Bierbauer Brewery in Canajoharie, New York. *Author's collection.*

In 1879, Carl Bierbauer sent F.X. Matt I to work at Louis Bierbauer's brewery in Canajoharie. F.X., who was twenty at the time, spent the next seven years expanding his knowledge of the brewing trade at this brewery. After the first year at the brewery, he became the brewmaster. F.X. returned to Utica and started the West End Brewing Company, which today produces Saranac beers.

On February 23, 1879, one hundred prominent local Germans assembled at the residence and brewery of Louis Bierbauer to congratulate him and his wife on their silver wedding anniversary.

An eight-horsepower engine and boiler were installed on April 25, 1883. Bierbauer had previously used actual horse power.

BIERBAUER BREWING COMPANY, 1904–20

In January 1904, the Bierbauer Brewing Company was incorporated. Louis Bierbauer, Louis H. Bierbauer and W.J. Roser were chosen as directors. In January 1906, the brewery was forced to cut ice from the canal instead of the river as it usually did due to the thinness of the ice on the river.

The brewery placed an order with the Brunswick Refrigerator Company of Brunswick, New Jersey, for a ten-ton ice machine on January 18, 1907. It

Bierbauer Brewery in Canajoharie, circa 1904. *Author's collection.*

was installed on March 1, after which the brewery no longer needed to cut ice on the river in the winter.

The brewery was discovered to be on fire shortly after 9:00 a.m. on February 7, 1907, and an alarm was sent in from the Arkell & Smiths sack factory. The fire company arrived quickly, and the fire was brought under control. The fire started in a cooper's room stove. In that section of the building, a number of bales of hops were stored, and the smoke and water did some damage to them. The loss was thought to be a couple hundred dollars and was covered by insurance with the H.R. Stafford agency. This was the first fire since the new fire alarm system was installed, and everybody was given the opportunity to try to locate the blaze by signal.

Louis Bierbauer died at his home at the age of eighty-six on September 24, 1918, after a brief illness. Ownership of the brewery passed to his son, Louis H. Bierbauer.

On Thursday morning, July 22, 1922, federal Prohibition agents raided the Bierbauer brewery and closed it down. It was being run at this time by Fred C. Roser of Cherry Valley and was to be closed for alleged violations of the federal Prohibition act in manufacturing beer of a prohibitive alcoholic strength. This was the first brewery in the district to be closed.

The brewery had been raided twice before by agents from the Syracuse office. The last time was on July 19, 1922, when agents alleged that they caught Roser and a man loading a truck with beer taken from the brewery cellar. This beer exceeded the allowable limit of one-half of 1 percent when tested.

The brewery was raided again on June 2, 1927. Agents reported that they found a modern brewery, bottling plant and facilities to speed production of beer on a large scale. They said that a new bottling machine had recently been installed. The agents did not indicate whether any arrests were made. They loaded up three trucks to capacity with beer and equipment.

Federal Prohibition agents again raided the old Bierbauer brewery on August 7, 1931, confiscated 1,500 barrels of alleged beer and arrested four men in the building at the time. The brewery had been operating for only a short time, according to people in the city.

The agents entered the building with no problem and arrested the four men they found there: Otto Osel, Andrew Melick, Howard Smith and Martin Steinberger, who was said to be the brewer. There was an underground passageway leading from the brewery property across upper Mill Street to a bottling plant. This building was also seized, and both buildings were locked up. In the brewery building, they found modern manufacturing equipment and mechanical cooling devices.

On August 8, the four men were arraigned before United States commissioner Lester Hubbard. They were charged with conspiracy, manufacturing and possession of intoxicating liquors and maintenance of a common nuisance. All pleaded not guilty, and the case was adjourned until September 9. The men posted $2,000 bail and were free to go.

The government had seized $100,000 worth of equipment in the raid. On February 9, 1932, William J. Roser (son-in-law of Louis Bierbauer) objected to the seizure and destruction of the equipment, claiming he had taken the property on a mortgage and did not know of its illegal use. The judge intimated that he would grant the petition; however, he reserved his decision pending the lawyers' filing of briefs.

The judge returned on February 26, 1932, with his decision that the equipment would be sold. The sale was set for April 18, 1932, at the brewery in Canajoharie. Since the brewery was closed, the Prohibition-enforcement department had guarded it with two men both night and day. The machinery was sold to Michael M. Dunn of Oneida.

On May 21, 1932, the assistant United States attorney asked for a judgment of $2,400 to be assessed against the Bierbauer Brewery Company officials. The brewing equipment was seized by federal agents.

Herman Roser fought the case, claiming he held a mortgage on the property. Roser's attorney contended that Roser should be held responsible for only the period of delay in the case caused by his fight to prevent the government's seizure of the property. The case went over pending further legal proof called for by the court that Roser should not stand the cost of two watchmen at five dollars a day each since and other costs.

Canajoharie Brewing Corporation, 1933–34

The Canajoharie Brewing Corporation was incorporated on March 22, 1933. The business had a capitalization of $75,000 and was authorized to engage in a general brewery business. Jacob Rutishauser, who had a guiding hand in the creamery interests of Canajoharie, was elected president. Nellis Shaver, who had charge of the Canajoharie United Cigars Store, was elected vice-president and would act as the active manager of the plant. C. Everett Dievendorf, who was active in real estate and insurance, was elected secretary and treasurer.

Ad from the *Gloversville Morning Herald*, September 1933.

The board of directors consisted of Louis H. Bierbauer and William J. Roser. Although Bierbauer was retired, he planned to devote considerable time to the brewery. This was done so that the corporation might have the benefit of the experience he gained during the many years he was associated with the organization under its previous management.

This group, along with interested backers in central New York and New York City, investigated many areas in New York State and decided that Canajoharie was the best location to start a new brewery. An analysis of the water located on the brewery property showed it to be especially adapted to the brewing of a specialty product that would be distinct in flavor and quality. The brand of this high-quality beer was to be known as "Mohawk," with an Indian head as a trademark.

A survey was made in the metropolitan district by the promoters of the brewery, and they were told that the entire output would be consumed in Greater New York. Several large hotels indicated that they were willing to contract for the full amount produced.

It was the intention of the new owners to remodel and increase the output of the brewery to meet this demand. The brewery was situated closer to the New York City market than the larger western breweries, and quicker deliveries would result. Lower transportation costs would also be realized.

The brewery had received its federal permit by July 1933 and resumed production immediately. Workmen had been remodeling the plant for quite a few weeks. William J. Kroll was chosen as brewmaster and became a permanent resident of the village. He resided on Phillips Avenue.

The brewery announced the return of Canajoharie Chief Lager Beer and King Hendrick Ale in September 1933. Both were available in bottles or on draught. Consumer tastes changed during Prohibition. The consumer now wanted a product that was more carbonated, like the sodas they had been drinking for the last thirteen years. The Canajoharie brewery was making its beer the old-fashioned way, and the product was not very carbonated. As a result of this, sales never reached a level that would let the brewery succeed.

The brewery filed a voluntary petition in bankruptcy without schedules on July 26, 1934. The financial statement would be filed within ten days. Jacob Rutishauser, as president, signed the petition, which was authorized by the board of directors on May 12. It was filed through Attorney Leonard Moore.

On July 21, 1934, schedules were filed with the clerk of the federal court. The schedules show liabilities of $28,606.49, including unsecured claims of $22,491.41, secured claims of $5,685.64, taxes of $429.44 and assets of $9,231.28.

Louis H. Bierbauer died at the Canajoharie hospital on Wednesday morning, February 24, 1937, at the age of seventy-two. He had been ill for about a year and had recently been moved to the hospital. He was survived by his wife, Helen; his daughter, Marie; and his son, William. He was buried in the Canajoharie Falls Cemetery.

On April 7, 1937, the old brewery was purchased from W.J. Roser by the Canajoharie Holding Corporation. William Jacobus of New York was president. The Canajoharie Holding Corporation was granted a charter by the secretary of state to establish a brewery and distillery business in Canajoharie. The company was incorporated with a capital of $20,000, divided into shares of $10 each. The directors were J. Jacques Stone, David Gerhardt and Joseph Meth, all of 80 Broad Street, New York.

The brewery was again up for sale in May 1938. Buyers were asked to call Mrs. W.J. Roser for details. Apparently, the Canajoharie Holding Corporation had failed, and Roser foreclosed on the property.

CHAPTER 3
CANASTOTA BREWERIES

2012–PRESENT

The village of Canastota is located in Madison County, thirty-two miles west of Utica. The historic name for the village is *KnisteStota*, and it was originally an Oneida Nation village. By the early 1800s, white settlers had largely supplanted the Indians. The village was incorporated in 1835 and was reorganized in 1870. Canastota was located on the Erie Canal, which was completed in 1825 and brought prosperity to the village. In those days, Canastota was known as an onion-growing town.

Today, Canastota has a population of approximately 4,100 people. It is home to the International Boxing Hall of Fame. Two world boxing champions came from Canastota: Carmen Basilio and Billy Backus. Each year at the induction ceremonies, famous boxing figures come to Canastota to celebrate the new inductees.

ERIE CANAL BREWING COMPANY, 2012–PRESENT

The Erie Canal Brewing Company was incorporated in Madison County, New York, on April 17, 2012. The owners are Sam Lanzafame and Jason Tedford. Tedford is the brewmaster. The brewery is located at 135 James Street in Canastota, just behind ZEMS Ice Cream & Mini Golf on Main Street. Tedford is leasing about 1,200 square feet of space in the building

A glass of Muleskinner Pale Ale from the Erie Canal Brewing Company in Canastota, New York. *Author's collection.*

from Rick Stevens, owner of ZEMS. The brewery will be able to expand into the remaining 6,000 square feet in the building if needed.

The brewery is very small and brews one hundred barrels per year. Each barrel is thirty-two gallons each. If this proves successful, Tedford has said he would expand to a couple thousand barrels annually. He makes just one barrel at a time, compared to the Empire Brewing Company, which makes seven barrels at a time, and Middle Ages Brewing in Syracuse, which makes thirty barrels at a time. The beer uses 100 percent local hops and barley. Currently, Tedford gets these raw materials from his partner, Sam Lanzafame, who owns a farm (BottePiena Farms) in Chittenango, New York.

Tedford has been brewing his own beer for more than twenty years. Lanzafame originally supplied Tedford with hops for his home brew, and as they shared the resulting brew, Lanzafame encouraged Tedford to go commercial. Tedford was a former CIO with Alliance Bank but lost his job when the company merged with NBT Bank. This allowed Tedford the opportunity to pursue brewing full time. The first brew produced by Tedford is a pale ale using two-row barley and cascade hops grown on Lanzafame's farm. The resulting brew is called Muleskinner Pale Ale and is named after the people who would walk with the mules as they towed boats down the canal. Once the brewery becomes established, Tedford plans to introduce a brown ale, but he is in no hurry.

A grand opening was held on August 11, 2013, as part of the village's and the Canastota Canal Town Corporation's dedication of two canal-themed murals and upgrades to the park at the corner of Peterboro and Canal Streets. In September 2013, Muleskinner Pale Ale was introduced at the Madison County Hop Fest, which celebrates the history and tradition of hop growing in the region.

The brewery will not have a tasting room like most of the other microbreweries currently operating, as Tedford wants to make sure he's supporting the local taverns with his products. The first place that Muleskinner Pale Ale was on tap was BG Buda's in Cazenovia on October 9, 2013. Three Pines in Canastota became the second place where you could get Muleskinner Pale Ale on tap on November 2, 2013.

On January 13, 2014, Jason Tedford gave a short history of beer and explained how he brews Muleskinner Pale Ale. This was held at the Canastota Public Library.

CHAPTER 4
CAZENOVIA BREWERIES

2011–PRESENT

C azenovia is located in Madison County, forty-two miles west of Utica. The village is on U.S. Route 20 and lies on the southeast shore of Cazenovia Lake. It was established in 1794 by a Dutch naval officer named John Lincklaen for the Holland Land Company. The village was named after an agent for the land company, Theophilus Cazenove. Cazenovia was incorporated in 1810.

Today, Cazenovia is home to Cazenovia College and has many historic sites that are listed on the National Register of Historic Places. It has a population of approximately 2,830.

EMPIRE FARMSTEAD BREWERY, INC., 2011–PRESENT

On January 13, 2011, the Empire Farmstead Brewery, Inc. was incorporated in Madison County by David Katleski. Katleski owns the Empire Brewpub located in Syracuse, New York. He is also the president of the New York State Brewers Association. On his farm in Madison County, he raises pumpkins used in his pumpkin ale, hops and the Wagyu beef served in the brewpub. His goal is to revive the region's hop culture. Once upon a time, the region was one of the largest hop-growing areas in the country. New York State grew 90 percent of the nation's supply until the late 1800s, when a hop blight wiped out several years of production. A move to dairy farming replaced hop farming.

Plans are in motion for the facility to be built in 2014, located at 1 Nickerson Street in Cazenovia, New York. At this brewery, Katleski plans to build two hop barns that would be largely decorative, forming the façade of the brewery. The brewery will be a twenty-thousand-square-foot production facility with a canning center flanked by hop trellises and vegetable gardens. The new facility will have a brewing capacity of sixty thousand barrels annually. The new brewery will take some of the pressure off the Empire Brewery in Syracuse. Tim Butler is the brewer at the Empire Brewery in Syracuse and will have a say in how the new brewery is constructed so that it runs well.

In early February 2013, the village board of trustees finalized the brewery's land annexation request. The brewery will be located on a twenty-two-acre lot on Route 13 across from the Lorenzo's Rippleton Schoolhouse. In May 2013, the village approved the location of the farm brewery based on the recently passed New York State law. The land was zoned residential, requiring an amendment to the village code. The village approved the changes in September 2013, giving the brewery the go-ahead to start building. Construction of the brewery will begin in 2014 with a goal of opening in the fall.

HENNEBERG BREWING COMPANY, 2012–PRESENT

In August 2013, John C. Henneberg received a farm brewery license from New York State. In April 2012, the Town of Cazenovia approved the brewery location. Henneberg was a home brewer who loved making beer and decided to take the next step and start making beer for a living. He started brewing in 2007 by making a pale ale from a kit that he bought online. That got him hooked, and so began his love affair with brewing beer. Henneberg and his wife opened a restaurant in Cazenovia on July 27, 2012, which has been very successful. It is located at 64 Albany Street and is called Henneberg Tavern. They feature local products from Good Nature Brewing, Empire Brewing, Harvest Moon Cidery, Owers Vineyard Wines and many others.

The Hennebergs own a ninety-seven-acre farm in New Woodstock, New York, just south of Cazenovia (seven miles) where the farm brewery will be located. They are currently growing and processing some of their own hops and grains used in their brews. The plan is to grow 100 percent of their raw materials in eight to ten years. This brewery will be much smaller than the

Logo for Henneberg's Winter Porter. *Author's collection.*

A beer bottle label from Henneberg Brewing, 2014. *Author's collection.*

John Henneberg, owner and brewer at Henneberg Brewing, 2013. *Author's collection.*

Empire Farmstead Brewery, which will also be located in Cazenovia. To start with, the brews will be available only in the Cazenovia area at the Henneberg Tavern. Henneberg hopes his will be the only brewery in the area, if not the state, to grow all the ingredients for its beer. In 2013, he grew three acres of barley, which yielded around two thousand pounds of barley. To keep up with demand, he buys his raw materials from the Bineyard (hops) in Cazenovia and from a farm in Canastota (barley). Henneberg malts his own base barley, which is a difficult process that is done by fewer than ten breweries in New York State. Henneberg currently brews around two barrels per week, which requires increased attention to detail to ensure that each batch is consistent. He brews four different beers from his own recipes: Farm House Pale Ale, Big Cock IPA, Gallagher's Irish Style Stout and Cazenovia Common (similar to Anchor Steam). The brews range from between 5.5 to 6.0 percent alcohol by volume. These are sold on tap at the Henneberg Tavern. In the future, he plans to upgrade his barrel system and produce about three hundred gallons per week (about fifteen thousand gallons annually).

A tasting room will be opened on his farm in the spring or early summer of 2014. He will sell kegs, six-packs and growlers from there. The brewery will be a stop on the Cazenovia Beverage Trail once it is up and running. In addition to the Henneberg Brewery, the trail consists of the Critz Farms Cidery, Owera Vineyards and the Empire Brewing Company. The beverage trail is a mutually beneficial relationship for all four partners, as well as a great boon for the local area.

CHAPTER 5
COOPERSTOWN BREWERIES

1816–PRESENT

Cooperstown is located forty-one miles to the southeast of Utica in Otsego County. The village was part of the Cooper patent, which Judge William Cooper purchased in 1785 from Colonel George Croghan. The village was established in 1786 and incorporated in 1807 as the Village of Otsego. Its name was changed to the Village of Cooperstown in 1812.

Presently, the village is the home to the National Baseball Hall of Fame and Museum, the Farmers' Museum, the Fenimore Art Museum, the Glimmerglass Opera and the New-York State Historical Association. The current population of Cooperstown is 1,850, although that number swells greatly during the summer with all of the visitors to the museums.

PATTEN BREWERY, 1816–40

Around 1816, David Patten built a brewery near the source of the creek on the road leading over the hill that came to be called Rum Hill. He was a native of Scotland and one of the original settlers in the area. Around 1833, David Patten built a stone house on Metcalf Hill in Pierstown. The house was located near Mount Otsego, on the road that, before the building of the state highways, was the direct route between Cooperstown and Richfield Springs. The stage lines of the olden days passed daily directly in front of the structure, as did the tallyhos and carriages of summer resort colonists and the more modest vehicles of permanent residents.

Patten sold the brewery to George T. Dalphin in the 1830s. Dalphin rebuilt the brewery and ran it until his death in 1840. After Patten died, his widow married Dalphin. The area where this brewery was located was then known as Pierstown. After 1840, the brewery buildings were converted into a barn to house the horses of patrons staying at the inn on Metcalf Hill.

Otsego Brewery, 1860s

By 1862, the village had a brewery called the Otsego Brewery, run by R.A. Lesley. It was said that he turned out superior pale and amber ale that was made from pure malt and No. 1 hops. I have been unable to find a street location for this brewery or any other information about it.

I have found mention of a Spafford's brewery on the south side of town but no suggestion of when it was in operation. Spafford also had a farm. A June 1887 newspaper article indicated that the old brewery, on the bank of the Susquehanna River, was quickly going to ruin. Much of the front wall had fallen in, and large cracks appeared in the south-side wall.

In the 1860s, Alben J. Wikoff was in the brewery business in Cooperstown. I don't know if he was connected with the Otsego Brewery, but he could have been. Wikoff was born in Pierstown on May 22, 1847, and lived his entire life in the area. After working in the brewery business in his early years, he became a farmer. The farm was located in Hyde Park. He died on December 29, 1926, at the Thanksgiving Hospital and was survived by six children.

Root & Beadle Brewery, 1817–Unknown

Sometime in the early 1800s, the company of Root and Beadle ran a brewery in the area. Elias Root built a house across the street from the brewery. A large bell was erected on the top of the Root malt house around 1817 and was a landmark of nineteenth-century Otsego County. The bell was saved from the ravages of fire when the malt house burned down in 1970. It was restored in 1976 and, at that time, was known as the "Kingsford Starch" bell. Around 1880, the house was purchased by Erastus F. Beadle, but it is unknown whether he also purchased the brewery. Erastus Beadle became famous for publishing Beadle's dime novels, which were treasured by every boy during that time.

Index Brewery, 1910

In June 1910, Paul Ott of New York City was in the Cooperstown area investigating the possibility of opening a brewery in the old Hope Mill at Index. Ott was the head of a company originally organized for the purpose of opening a brewery in Oneonta.

The company had already purchased all the equipment needed for the proposed brewery. It was understood at that time that the officials of the electric road were interested in the Index proposition. The idea for a brewery here was scrapped, and Ott went back to New York City.

Phoenix Brewery, 1913–15

In August 1913, a Cooperstown syndicate composed of Martin Moakler, James J. Byard Jr., W.D. Burditt and Jay D. Wilson purchased real estate of the old Fenimore Mills at Phoenix Mills for $3,900 at an auction sale. Moakler stated that he and his partners would incorporate in the very near future, and it was their idea to begin the operation of a brewery there in the fall. They were also considering selling the property to someone else for the right price.

Moakler also stated that there had already been made two applications by manufacturing concerns for options on the plant, provided the proposed freight rate question should be carried by the vote of the town. It was thought that this would be a practical industry for this location inasmuch as it is centrally situated in the hop-raising section of Otsego County. In addition to a possible brewery, several potential buyers of the property wanted to start a silk mill or a shoe factory.

For most of his life, Martin Moakler grew hops. At one time, he owned nine hop farms. He was the largest dealer in the area and amassed quite a fortune. He was personal friends with August A. Busch, founder of the Anheuser-Busch Brewing Company. The hop blight wiped out most of his business, and as a result, he retired. He began to deal in property as a means to keep busy. On September 9, 1954, he celebrated his ninetieth birthday and was in good health.

In early 1915, Moakler sold the property to a group, but it did not indicate what it was going to do with it. The site was not made into a brewery. Moakler said his plans were to operate a motor bus company in Cooperstown and also to fix up several houses he had bought when he purchased the mill for rentals.

BREWERY OMMEGANG, 1997–PRESENT

Brewery Ommegang was established in 1997 on a 140-acre former hop farm located approximately six and a half miles south of Cooperstown, New York, on Highway 33. It was the first farmstead brewery founded in the United States in more than a century. It was started by the husband-wife team of Don Feinberg and Wendy Littlefield with investment from some of Belgium's premier brewing companies. The couple was recognized as Belgian beer experts and co-owners of Vanberg & DeWulf, importers of traditional Belgian ales since 1982. Partners in the joint brewing venture included the proprietors of two of Belgium's leading independents—Michael Moorgat, president of the Moorgat Brewery, and Theo Vervloet, brewer at DeSmedt (makers of Affligem)—as well as Ben Gevaert, an independent brewing consultant. The brewer chosen to brew the products is a Belgian native and a graduate of Louvain's Institute of Brewing Studies who arrived in the winter of 1996. Construction was begun in 1996 and was finished in May 1997. The brewery was built to resemble a Belgian farmhouse. The brewery uses a forty-barrel Falco-Steineker Brewhouse. Brewing began immediately, and a grand opening was held in mid-summer 1997. The brewery employed eight people in the beginning.

The brewery uses time-honored Belgian brewing techniques like open fermentation and warm cellaring to create its flavorful ales. It uses Belgian ale yeast and specialty malts and Czech and American specialty hops and adds spices such as coriander, sweet orange peel, ginger, star anise and grains of paradise (a peppery West African spice).

In 2005, Duvel Moortgat bought complete ownership of Ommegang and launched Duvel USA. Since its purchase, the brewery has been expanded and has become known for its large festivals and summer concert series.

The Brewery Ommegang sign in Cooperstown, New York, 2010. *Author's collection.*

Brewery Ommegang from road, 2014. *Author's collection.*

Brewery Ommegang storage tanks, 2014. *Author's collection.*

Demand was so high in 2008 that some of Ommegang's ales were being brewed in Belgium and shipped to the United States. To alleviate this problem, the brewery installed four new fermenting tanks.

In 2009, the brewery began another expansion of its facility to keep up with demand for its Belgian ales. The first phase would construct an eight-thousand-square-foot warehouse. Before construction of the new warehouse, Ommegang had to warehouse its products off-site in New Jersey and California. Its ales are bottle conditioned, and as soon as that process was complete, the ale was trucked to the warehouses out of state. The new warehouse eliminated the need for this and provided additional warm cellaring space for the bottle conditioning. It also freed up space for production. The next phase of the expansion created a retail store, a restaurant, office space and a new bottling hall. The expansion added five jobs and cost $1.8 million.

All the investments in buildings and equipment over the last few years have given the brewery a capacity of 100,000 barrels per year. At this stage, it produces around 40,000 barrels per year, with 55 percent of that being draft and 45 percent bottled. During this time period, Ommegang has strived to maintain the Belgium tradition of brewing, which requires a slow and deliberate process. As an example, Ommegang brews are given a little sugar at bottling and then aged for ten days at eighty degrees Fahrenheit.

This requires a warm cellaring space, which was a bottleneck until the 2009 addition of a warm cellar.

The brewery creates six award-winning Belgian-style ales year round, as well as at least four seasonal and specialty ales. The year-round ales include Witte White Ale, Belgian Pale Ale, Rare Vos Amber Ale, Hennepin Farmhouse Saison Ale, Ommegang Abbey Dubbel Ale and Three Philosophers Abbey Quadruple Ale. Each ale has won awards and is quite unique.

Ommegang ales are distributed throughout the United States and have a large following. Justin Forsythe and Scott Veltman are the current brewers. Their home-brewing pasts have prepared them to craft the Belgian-style ales for which Ommegang is known.

Located directly behind the brewery in a separate building is Café Ommegang, which has an attached gift shop. The café has a bar and table sittings for visitors and a beer garden located to one side where visitors can eat and drink outdoors. It has ten draft lines available and serves other Belgian-style ales in bottles. The food served is Belgian-themed. Tastings and tours are offered every day except major holidays. It is open from noon to 5:00 or 7:00 p.m. depending on the day. Tours are held every half hour until 4:40 p.m. The brewery's website gives the most current information (ommegang.com).

During the year, the brewery hosts several festivals, with its Belgium Comes to Cooperstown Beer Festival, held in mid-summer, being the most popular. From May through September, it has a concert series that is held outdoors on the brewery grounds. In past years, Lyle Lovett, Levon Helm, REO Speedwagon and Huey Lewis have performed.

In January 2010, brewmaster Phil Leinhart and the entire Ommegang brew staff kicked off an innovation program that created six ales, four of which were new to complement Ommegang's year-round ale offerings. Every two months, the brewery will release one of the brews, which will be offered in 750-milliliter bottles and sixth-barrel kegs. These ales will be released nationally in limited quantities of roughly two thousand cases and the equivalent volume in sixth-barrel kegs. The ales produced were, in order: Ommegang Chocolate Indulgence Stout, Ommegang BPA (Belgian-style pale ale), Ommegang Tripel, Ommegang Sour Ale, Ommegang Scotch Ale and Ommegang Adoration. The brewery also developed six experimental, exclusive and small-batch ales, which were available only on-site. These were not for sale but were available for sampling by visitors to the brewery.

In 2012, Ommegang partnered with HBO to produce a series of new beers inspired by the HBO drama *Game of Thrones*. The first offering was called Iron Throne, a blond ale that was released on the March 31, 2013 debut of season three of *Game of Thrones*. Iron Throne was available nationally in 750-milliliter bottles and on draft. The brewmaster tasked with developing this brew was Phil Leinhart, who created a delicate but piercing golden blond ale with Noble hops.

Also in 2013, Ommegang and HBO partnered again to produce Black Stout for HBO's *Game of Thrones* series. This was the second offering and was available in September 2013. It was offered in 750-milliliter bottles and sixth-barrel kegs. In 2014, Ommegang produced Fire & Blood Red Ale as its latest offering for the *Game of Thrones* series.

The brewery partnered with Hurricane Sandy–damaged Barrier Brewing on Long Island in late 2012 to create Barrier Relief Ale, a Belgian-style IPA. Ommegang brewed four hundred kegs of beer, which were sold in Barrier's market in New York City and the surrounding area. The profits from the sale of the beer were used by Barrier Brewing to help toward repairing the $100,000 worth of damages.

In October 2013, Brewery Ommegang's parent company, Duvel Moortgat of Belgium, purchased the Boulevard Brewing Company of Kansas City, Missouri. Boulevard Brewing Company is a major craft brewery in the Midwest. It produces 128,000 barrels per year compared to Ommegang's 40,000 barrels per year.

COUNCIL ROCK BREWERY, 2012–PRESENT

In 2012, brewer Roger Davidson decided to start a brewery in the Cooperstown area. A location was chosen on State Route 28, just a half mile south of the hamlet of Index. This location is approximately five miles south of Cooperstown and is located just across the road from the Cooperstown Fun Park. The site that was chosen is a one-story building that sits back from the road. When it originally opened up for business, the brewery was quite difficult to find. It had a small sign located near the road, mixed in with other business signs, and the building itself sat a distance from the road behind a clump of pine trees. The signage on the building was also quite small.

Prior to starting the brewpub, Davidson had been a teacher and became interested in home brewing in 2003. He started with extracts before moving to all-grain brewing. As his brewings grew, he and his wife decided to open a brewpub.

A Council Rock Brewery business card. *Author's collection.*

In late February 2012, Davidson announced that they were in the final phases of setting up and licensing the new brewery. On April 30, they received approval from the New York State Department of Health for their kitchen. Upon receiving final approval, brewing began in order to prepare for the opening.

Davidson installed a three-barrel pilot system that can brew up to fifty-gallon batches at a time. Typically, they brew one- to three-barrel batches. Annual production is three hundred barrels at this time. Their standard brews are Goldenrod Ale, Full Nelson Ale, Sleeping Lion Red Ale, Leatherstocking Brown Ale, Sunken Island Scotch Ale and Heffeweizen. Since opening the brewery, many seasonal and limited offerings have been made. The various brews have an alcohol-by-volume range from 4.5 percent in the Goldenrod Ale to 9.0 percent in the Sunken Island Scotch Ale. They usually offer a guest brew on tap from other micros.

The Council Rock Brewery is named after an actual rock that sits in the water where Otsego Lake meets the Susquehanna River in Cooperstown. In March 2013, the brewery started offering growlers, allowing patrons to take the beer home to enjoy.

On May 5, 2012, the brewery conducted a soft opening with limited hours and food. On May 24, it started to build a beer garden and encouraged people to come and help. By the twenty-seventh, the parking lot lines were being painted, and fencing was being put around the beer garden. The brewery

Council Rock Brewery in Cooperstown, 2013. *Author's collection.*

A glass and bottle of Council Rock Brewery Ale. *Author's collection.*

received ten different craft sodas from Cooper's Cave, which have become regular offerings at the brewery.

Council Rock brewer Roger Davidson got together with Cooperstown Brewing brewer Wes Nick in August 2012 to produce a brew together. They produced Wings of Darkness Black Lager, which was quite successful.

In 2013, the brewery expanded into the shop located behind the brewery to gain more space. It installed a new kitchen in the expanded part of the brewery,

Right: Beer coasters from two microbreweries. *Author's collection.*

Below: A selection of Council Rock beers. *Courtesy of Chopsticks Optional.*

Wes Nick (Cooperstown Brewing's brewer) and Roger Davidson (owner and brewer of Council Rock Brewing) in 2013. *Author's collection.*

increasing its capability. Currently, the brewery has approximately ten barstools and a few tables where you can grab a sandwich and have some beer, wine and soda. It is open from 11:00 a.m. to 9:00 p.m. every day. It is also installing two new lager tanks to try to keep up with demand.

Business is going so well that Davidson decided he could not do the festival circuit in 2014 because he was having a hard time keeping up with demand and needed to be at the brewery full time. The beer is available only at the brewpub at this time.

CHAPTER 6
FORT PLAIN BREWERIES
1878–1904

T he village of Fort Plain is located thirty-nine miles to the east of Utica in Montgomery County. The village was first settled in 1738, when the governor of New York built a stone house for his sons to use. Other early settlers were largely Palatine Germans. A fort was constructed in 1776 to keep the women and children safe while the men were off fighting the war. Fort Plain was incorporated in 1832 and experienced an economic boom with the opening of the Erie Canal. The village was named after the fort. It is the birthplace of the first black professional baseball player, Bud Fowler. Fowler appeared in an exhibition game with a team from Lynn, Iowa, in 1878.

Today, the village and area are home to a large number of Amish. This group of people is better known to be from southern Pennsylvania and Ohio than New York. Montgomery County now has one of the largest Amish populations in the country. The current population of Fort Plain is 2,320.

FORT PLAIN BREWERY, 1878–97

John Beck was born in 1833 in Germany. He arrived in America when he was a young man in the early 1870s. He settled in Fort Plain and started a brewery in 1878 that was quite successful. Beck brewed lager beer exclusively. The brewery was located on Beck Street, and all the buildings were of wooden construction. The property included five

Ad from the *Little Falls City Directory*, 1891.

connected buildings, three of which fronted Beck Street. The buildings on the street contained a one-story icehouse, a one-story storage building and a larger, two-story storage building. The brewhouse was a two-and-a-half-story building attached to the larger storage building. The malt mill was contained in a two-story building attached to the brewhouse. Beneath the brewery, there were large cellars that kept the lager beer cool. The property also contained two other one-story icehouses and a detached wooden dance hall. A detached barn housed the brewery wagons and horses. The brewery ran on steam power, using coal to make the steam. The lights in the brewery were fueled by coal oil. The brewery was quite successful during the nineteen years it was run by Beck.

Over the years, a large picnic area was created on the brewery property, which became very popular and far outlasted the brewery itself. The area was known as "Beck's Grove." Beck retired in 1897, selling his brewery to Berthold Matt (Matte). John Beck died on February 28, 1906, at the age of seventy-three. He had been in ill health for the previous two years but took a turn for the worse a couple days before his death.

PELICAN BREWERY, 1897—1904

When Berthold Matt (Matte) took over the brewery in 1897, he changed the name of the brewery to the Pelican Brewery. Many people also started to call the brewery the Berthold Matte Brewery. The names seemed to be quite interchangeable.

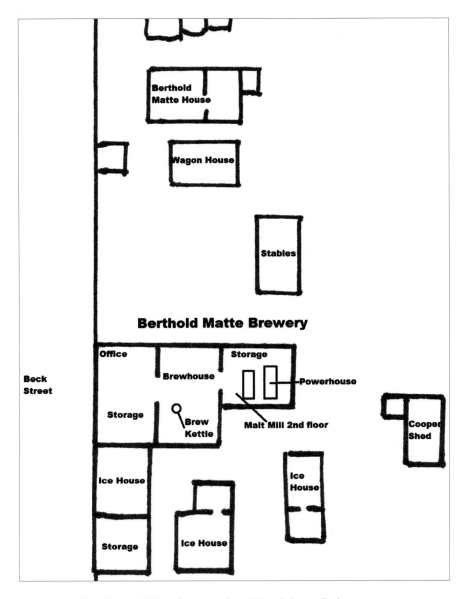

A drawing of the Berthold Matte Brewery, circa 1901. *Author's collection.*

In 1901, the brewery had five attached buildings, three of which faced Beck Street. These buildings contained an office, icehouse and two storage areas. The icehouse and one of the storage buildings were each one story. The building containing the office and other storage area was two stories.

Attached to the rear of this two-story building was a two-and-a-half-story brewhouse. Attached to the rear of the brewhouse was a two-story malt mill. The property also contained two stand-alone icehouses, a stable, a wagon shop and a cooper shed. All the buildings were constructed primarily of wood. The brewery was powered by steam, which was generated by using coal as fuel. Lighting for the brewery was done using coal oil.

Matt was not successful in running the business. During his tenure, he made no improvements to the brewery buildings or processes. As a result, the business started to fail and was finally closed in 1904. It was never reopened. However, the picnic area, Beck's Grove, continued to be very popular up to the start of World War II.

After the brewery closed, Berthold Matt worked for the West End Brewery as its district representative in the Fort Plain area. Matt was in that position until around 1941, when he was transferred to the main office in Utica. He died on November 9, 1942, at the age of eighty-one after an illness of about two weeks.

By 1924, the brewery property was owned by Joseph Pickard. On June 26, 1924, eight federal agents from Albany raided the brewery when the owner was not present. They believed that it was one of the hidden sources of supply for the Mohawk Valley.

They forced their way into the cellar of the brewery, where they discovered 340 cases of alleged beer in bottles, 440 half barrels of hard cider and a large quantity of grain and mash. Pickard and Rhodes Sagwin, an employee, were arrested later and taken before United States commissioner Frank Shawl at Little Falls. The value of the confiscated booze was said to be $25,000.

Pickard appeared before the commissioner and gave bail for appearance at a future hearing. Later, Pickard indicated that it was true that a number of barrels of cider were found, along with a few half barrels and cases of alleged beer. However, there was no truth regarding the 440 half barrels of cider and 340 cases of alleged beer. The large quantity of grain and mash discovered was in reality a half barrel of oats, used for chicken feed.

The previous fall, Pickard had bought the sweet cider directly from the manufacturer and then stored it in the brewery's cold cellars. It was never offered to the public or altered in any way since it was initially stored. The brewery building itself contained no equipment that could be used in the manufacture of beer or hard cider.

Pickard was fined $425 in September at the special term of federal court for violating the Volstead Act. He also lost all the cider and alleged beer. Sometime after 1925, Philip Freebold purchased the property.

Freebold ran a motor trucking business at the time. On Friday, September 25, 1931, he held an auction in the old brewery barn. He was auctioning off a full car of cattle and offered to sell any others that people brought in for a 7 percent commission.

In October 1933, Charles Swartz purchased the old brewery from Philip Freebold. The property included a grove and dance pavilion in addition to the brewery buildings. Swartz ran a place at Bull Run. In August 1932, he was arrested by federal agents when they found twenty-four pints of alleged beer at his establishment. He secured bail and was released. Swartz was probably thinking he could start the brewery back up, but in the end, he had overextended himself. He filed for bankruptcy, which was granted on August 3, 1938. As a creditor, Philip Freebold regained control of the brewery property.

Freebold sold the property to Ray Steenburgh in early 1940. On Sunday, June 9, 1940, at 2:45 a.m., the old dance hall building caught fire. The fire was of unknown origin and gutted the building. Steenburgh had just recently renovated the upstairs into two apartments and was living in one of them. The first floor was a garage.

Mrs. Steenburgh was aroused by the mewing of a cat, and when she opened the back door that led to a storeroom, flames shot out at her. She called the fire department, which arrived quickly, and the fire was declared out by 8:00 a.m. The interior of the building was charred, and most of the furniture in the two apartments was burned. The cat that perhaps saved Mrs. Steenburgh's life perished in the blaze. However, firemen were able to save the cat's four kittens. The blaze was believed to have started in the storeroom. The building was partly covered by insurance. The dance hall was repaired, and Philip Freebold again came into possession of the brewery property.

On November 24, 1944, it was announced that the Village of Fort Plain had bought the property for $1,800 from Freebold. Following proposed improvements, the property was leased to the fire department, which regulated the activities held there. One barn and the dance hall were preserved. The brewery building and the other barn were dismantled and removed. Today, the cold cellars are all that remain of the brewery, and these are not accessible to the public.

CHAPTER 7

GARRATTSVILLE BREWERIES

2005–PRESENT

G arrattsville is a very small village located thirty-nine miles south of Utica in Otsego County along Route 51. The village was named for John Garratt. He and his wife were carried into captivity by Indians and held for seven years. After that, they returned to their cabin and restarted their lives. In 1878, Garrattsville had two churches, three general stores, a hardware store, a sawmill and gristmill, a hotel, a wagon shop and five blacksmiths. Artemas Holdredge, a cheese manufacturer in Garrattsville, invented the concept of putting cheese in rectangular boxes instead of the usual round boxes to make shipping and storage easier. The village was a thriving place in the early years. Today, the population of the village is only 253. In December 2010, the post office was closed.

BUTTERNUTS BEER AND ALE BREWERY, 2005–PRESENT

Chuck Williamson and his partner, Leo Bongiorno, bought an old 120-acre dairy farm with the intention of converting it into a brewery in 2002. The brewery is located at 4021 Highway 51 in Garrattsville, New York. Williamson said at the time:

> Our image and our intention with the Butternuts brand was to kind of take that "pretense" of craft beer off the table. At the time, especially in the late 1990s

early 2000s, there was a definite divide between the macro beer drinker and the micro beer drinker. The macro beer drinker felt alienated, so they would just say I don't like the stuff, because I can't approach it. And its human nature, if you're not familiar with it, you just want to say no. So we wanted to try and break that boundary down, and say, hey this is beer, but it is fun. It's good beer, but don't be so serious, don't be overly serious about it, give it a try.

They set about renovating the old cow barn, which took until 2005. Besides installing the usual brew kettles and storage tanks, they also installed a canning line. This is quite unusual, as it is more typical for a microbrewery to install a bottling line. Williamson is the brewmaster. The name "Butternuts" comes from the Butternut Mountains where the brewery is located. Brewing started in 2005, with sales beginning in 2006.

The brewery's first brew was Porkslap Pale Ale, followed by Heinnieweisse Weissebier, Snapperhead IPA and Moo Thunder Stout. These four ales are offered year round and are available in cans and kegs. The brewery has

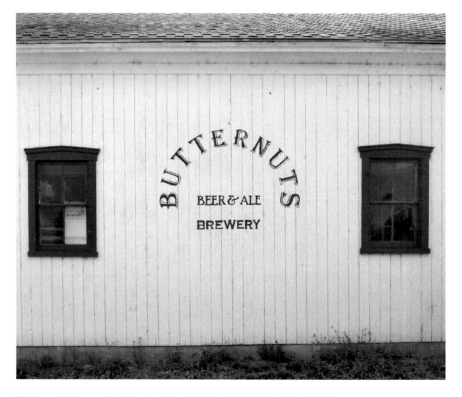

Butternuts Brewery in Garrettsville, New York, 2010. *Author's collection.*

also produced Brutus Imperial IPA, Butternuts ESP (Extra Special Porkslap), Butternuts Trappist Ale, County Gold Saison, Doppelbock, Double Moo Thunder, Landis Harvest Ale and Pelham Bay IPA. These are seasonal offerings and are available only in kegs.

The main Butternuts beers are sold in fourteen states along the eastern seaboard, with Porkslap Pale Ale representing 60 percent of the sales. Bongiorno left the company in 2007 to pursue other interests

In the summer of 2011, the brewery was thinking about expanding to keep up with sales and to be able to increase its distribution. Butternuts presented a plan to the Schoharie County supervisors to purchase the old Guilford Mills in Cobleskill, New York. The mill has been vacant since 2001 and was in need of some repairs. The brewery would be willing to spend $1.2 million for the building repairs, along with $910,000 in equipment to get the facility up and running. However, it would need concessions from the county. The county supervisors and the brewery spent the next couple months reviewing the plan.

By the end of October 2011, the county agreed to not entertain other buyers for the property, giving the brewery exclusive rights to purchase the property for sixty days. A spinoff company was formed called Longhouse LLC to pursue this project. The brewery needed exclusive rights to be able to apply for a grant that would be part of the funding to buy the building. The purchase price of the factory was set at $2.5 million, and the brewery

Butternuts Brewery in Garrettsville, 2012. *Author's collection.*

Butternuts Brewery beer cans. *Author's collection.*

asked the county to hold the mortgage for ten years at an interest rate of 5 percent. The banker representing the brewery also indicated that the payments would be delayed for thirty-five months into the contract, and instead of regular tax payments, the brewery would make payments in lieu of taxes to be negotiated on the purchase price.

The brewery estimated that it would employ up to sixty people and would get tax credits for creating these jobs over the next four years and maybe one hundred jobs after ten years. The Butternuts brewery has grown by more than 50 percent a year since it began. Getting this building would satisfy the immediate and long-term needs of the brewery. The brewery has less than 10,000 square feet of production space, and the Guilford mill would add approximately 460,000 square feet. Some of that space would be sublet to other businesses.

After many extensions to the deadline, the county finally decided to seek other buyers for the mill in 2013. The brewery had been unable to get the deal completed for various reasons, although it was still trying. The county supervisors said Longhouse LLC/Butternuts could still pursue purchasing the property. In December 2013, Butternut executives were looking into developing a relationship with the State University at Cobleskill that would allow firms moving into Guilford Mills to enjoy tax-free status under Governor Andrew Cuomo's Start-Up New York program.

Beer coasters from three microbreweries. *Author's collection.*

As of this writing (2014), Butternuts is still pursuing opening a brewery in the Cobleskill area. This brewery would be a one-hundred-barrel production system capable of brewing Butternuts' major products and also contract brewing for other breweries. Presently, Butternuts brews for Spider Bite Beer Company, Evil Genius Beer Company and Ruckus Brewing Company.

Butternuts opened a brewpub at a nearby golf course, Butternut Golf & Valley Recreation in New Berlin, which it purchased and operates. At this location, there is a ten-gallon nano-system (small-batch brewing system). As of 2014, the brewery ranks as the fiftieth largest microbrewery in the United States. The brewery produced around eight thousand barrels of ale in 2012.

When the big brewery opens, Williamson will have a nano-brewery (in New Berlin), a packaging brewery (in the Cobleskill area) and two micros (in Garrettsville and Milford). This will allow him to experiment on all levels of brewing. The tasting room at the Butternuts Brewery is open daily from noon to 6:00 p.m.

CHAPTER 8
HAMILTON BREWERIES

2012–PRESENT

Hamilton, New York, is a small village located in Madison County, approximately thirty miles southwest of Utica. It has a population of 4,240 and is home to Colgate University. Hamilton was originally inhibited by Indians of the Iroquois League. The original name for Hamilton was "Payne's Settlement," after Elisha Payne, who settled in the area in 1795. In the beginning, salt was the accepted form of currency. The area flourished in the early 1800s from extensive crop exports to Europe and from the opening, in 1808, of the Skaneateles Turnpike, which connected the village to western New York. The village became incorporated as the Village of Hamilton in 1812, named in honor of Alexander Hamilton. Hamilton's brewing history is recent, with the Good Nature Brewing Company being formed in January 2012. Any early breweries were small home operations that did not leave any records of their existence.

GOOD NATURE BREWING COMPANY, 2012–PRESENT

In January 2012, Carrie Blackmore and Matt Whalen formed the Good Nature Brewing Company. They started with a two-barrel system, but this proved to be too small for the amount of business they did right from the start. In the first four months, they exceeded their three-year projections. By the summer of that year, they had installed a seven-barrel system made

Good Nature Brewing's logo. *Author's collection.*

by Global Tanks. The new system uses electricity instead of gas or oil like many breweries because the village of Hamilton has an electric cooperative. Annual production is currently at four hundred barrels. The 1,700-square-foot facility is located at 37 Milford Street in Hamilton, New York. They handcraft all-natural ales brewed with local ingredients. The ales are unfiltered and contain no artificial additives or adjuncts.

Matt Whalen is the brewmaster. He was trained as a chef and pays close attention to detail when crafting his recipes. Marc Fishel is the assistant brewer. All operations are done in-house. Year round, they produce six different ales: Good Nature Blonde, American Pale Ale, India Pale Ale, American Brown Ale, Chicory Mocha Porter and The Nor'Easter. They have also produced eight seasonal ales: Chamomile Honey White, Belgian IPA, CNY Harvest, The Great Chocolate Wreck, The Warm N' Toasty,

Good Nature Brewing in Hamilton, New York. *Author's collection.*

Good Nature Brewing pint glass and growler. *Author's collection.*

Matt Whalen, owner and brewmaster at Good Nature Brewing in Hamilton, 2013. *Author's collection.*

Solstice Oat Stout, Rabbit In the Rye-Pa and Solera Bourbon-Aged Porter. The alcohol by volume for these brews ranges from a low of 4.5 percent (Good Natured Blonde) to 10.0 percent (The Great Chocolate Wreck). In 2012, the brewery produced seven hundred barrels of ale. Most of the ales are available on draft and occasionally in 750-milliliter bottles for specialty ales. If the brew is available on draft, you can get a growler to go.

The brewery received its farm brewery license in early 2013 and added two new fermenting tanks to keep up with demand. In July 2013, it brewed its first sour beer, called Sour Bourbon Brown Ale.

In 2013, it moved its tasting room from the brewery building to a building at 8 Broad Street in downtown Hamilton. This is open to the public on Tuesdays through Saturdays, as well as the occasional Sunday. You can check when the tasting room is open on the brewery's website (www. goodnaturebrewing.com). With the opening of this new tasting room, the brewery itself is not currently open to the public, although tours are given by appointment. Every Friday or Saturday, the tasting room has live music from 9:00 p.m. to midnight. In the spring of 2014, the brewery started offering its Blonde, Brown, IPA and Annie Imperial IPA beers in twenty-two-ounce bomber bottles.

CHAPTER 9

HERKIMER BREWERIES
1861–1896

The village of Herkimer is located sixteen miles east of Utica in Herkimer County. The village was named after the Herkimers, early Palatine Germans who came to this area in 1723. General Nicholas Herkimer was the most famous and died from his wounds at the Battle of Oriskany during the Revolutionary War. Over its history, the village was attacked many times by Indians, French and English. The village was incorporated in 1807, and its charter was amended in 1832 to enlarge the village. It was reorganized in 1875. Herkimer runs along the Mohawk River and the West Canada River. Like other villages in the Mohawk Valley, the Erie Canal, New York State Thruway and U.S. Route 5 run through the village, enabling it to grow over the years. The village is the county seat for Herkimer County. The current population of Herkimer is 7,740.

HELLMICK BREWERY, 1861–78

In 1861, Philip Hellmick started a lager beer brewery at 10 Washington Street in the village of Herkimer. Hellmick was born in Germany in 1825 and arrived in this country in 1859. By 1874, the brewery had produced 307 barrels for lager. In 1875, this total increased to 349 barrels. This was the high point of production for the brewery under Hellmick. Hellmick ran the brewery until March 4, 1878, when he sold it to Anna M. Goldsmith

(Goldschmidt), whose husband (Francis) ran a brewery and grocery store in Rome. He sold the brewery for $4,000. After selling the brewery, Hellmick entered into the saloon business at 21 Main Street in Herkimer. Hellmick died in 1904 at age seventy-nine, as did his wife, Christina, at age sixty-one.

FORT DAYTON BREWERY, 1878–92

The Goldsmiths purchased the brewery site on March 4, 1878. The brewery, located at 10 Washington Street, was renamed the Fort Dayton Brewery by Anna Goldsmith in honor of Fort Dayton, an old Revolutionary War fort. She expanded the brewery shortly after taking over—to a five-hundred-barrel capacity. Anna Goldsmith lived next to the brewery at 8 Washington Street, along with Francis Goldsmith, brewmaster at the brewery. She was born in Germany in 1821. Her maiden name was Anna Marie Werstline. She immigrated to America with Francis in 1854, and they were married in Buffalo, where they resided for a short time. The couple moved in 1856 to Rome, where Francis started a brewery. In 1877, they relocated to Herkimer, where Anna bought the brewery owned by Philip Hellmick. Around 1901, she moved to Utica with her husband. She died on December 6, 1904, at the age of eighty-three, at St. Elizabeth's Home after a lingering illness. Henry Goldsmith was employed as the superintendent at the brewery, and John Goldsmith was working as an agent.

At this time, the brewery consisted of several attached buildings. The front section was a two-story dwelling that was used as a saloon. Attached directly behind it was the two-story brewhouse. The brew kettle and malt room were located on the first floor. The second floor contained raw material storage. Directly north of the brewhouse was a one-story attached engine room. Finally, a one-story icehouse was attached to the rear of the brewhouse. The Goldsmith residence was the first house directly north of the brewery. The brewery was rebuilt during the summer of 1885 to modernize it, and by August, it was again brewing.

On December 7, 1890, Henry Goldsmith died in Syracuse. John Goldsmith became the superintendent at the brewery following Henry's passing. In January 1893, Anna Goldsmith leased her brewery to Peter Yannes (Yanner), of Luzerne County, Pennsylvania, for five years. She moved to 429 North Washington Street and entered into the grocery and provision business. Yannes changed the name of the brewery to the City Brewery.

On October 5, 1908, Francis Goldsmith died in St. Elizabeth's Hospital after an illness of several months. Francis had moved to Utica and, since 1903, lived at the hospital, where he worked as a volunteer. Francis was born in Bavaria, Germany, in 1822. He was eighty-six when he died. John Goldsmith passed away on June 17, 1918, following an illness that confined him to a hospital for four years. He was fifty-eight years old.

City Brewery, 1893–96

Yannes made some improvements to the brewery after taking over. Under his direction, the brewery produced lager beer, ale, porter, soda water and all kinds of soft drinks. He also managed a bar on the premises. Yannes ran the brewery until sometime in 1893, when he defaulted on his lease and the brewery reverted to Goldsmith. A small one-story attached building was added to the

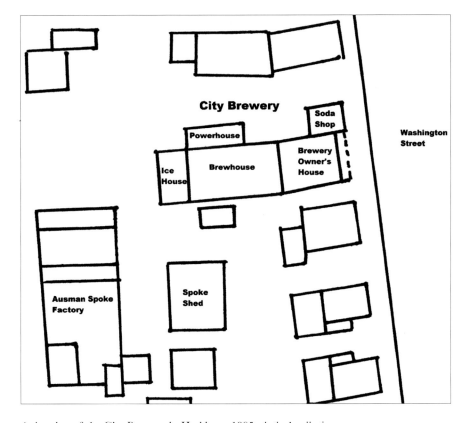

A drawing of the City Brewery in Herkimer, 1895. *Author's collection.*

CITY BREWERY!

PETER YANNES, Proprietor.

Having purchased the Fort Dayton Brewery in Herkimer and improved the same, is prepared to furnish the finest

=:= SODA WATER =:=

and all kinds of soft drinks to be found and will guarantee all his goods. All orders by mail, or otherwise, will be attended to. We manufacture the best

Lager Beer, Ale and Porter.

Ad from the *Herkimer County Directory*, 1893.

north side of the dwelling house in 1893. This building was added by Yannes, and he used it to sell his soda.

In 1894, Otto Lambert succeeded Yannes and leased the brewery for a couple years. Not much information has been found about him or what changes he made to the brewery. By 1896, the brewery had gone out of business, thus ending the manufacture of beer in Herkimer.

In September 1897, James J. Grace, formerly brewmaster for the National Brewing Company in Syracuse, leased the brewery and planned to operate it as an ale brewery. He would make ale and porter only and would begin operating the brewery without delay. He moved to a house on Church Street in Herkimer. These plans never proceeded any further.

The property was not in use as a brewery in 1900. The dwelling house in front of the old brewery was a grocery store, and the one-story addition was used as a candy store. On October 31, 1902, the property of the brewery was sold under foreclosure by attorney E.B. Mitchell, acting as referee. The mortgage on the property was held by a Mrs. Johnson of Utica. The brewery was purchased by Dr. D.M. Davendorf of Herkimer for $2,700.

CHAPTER 10
ILION BREWERIES
1861–1898

The village of Ilion is located twelve miles east of Utica in Herkimer County. Ilion was first settled in 1725 by German Palatines under the Burnetsfield Patent. It was called New London to begin with but was named Ilion in 1843. In 1816, Eliphalet Remington created his first gun at a forge located in Ilion Gorge. The people of the village wanted to name it Remington, but Eliphalet was against that choice. The Erie Canal ran through the village and helped it expand. The village was incorporated in 1852. Besides making guns, Remington also made farm equipment, bicycles and typewriters. Since the early 1800s, Remington businesses have been the major employer in the area. Today, Remington Arms is the top gun maker in the United States. The current population of Ilion is 8,050.

MOHAWK VALLEY BREWERY, 1861–67

The earliest mention of a brewery in Ilion was in 1861. The Mohawk Valley Brewery was formed by J. Myers & Co. It produced XX and XXX Pale and Amber Ales. The X in front of the ale name signified how much alcohol the product contained. Triple X contained more alcohol than double X. Peter Vidvard from Utica was one of its agents.

The brewery was located directly on the Erie Canal, a half mile from the New York Central Railroad station. The building was brick with a brick malt house attached that had a capacity of ten thousand barrels. There was another malt house adjoining with a capacity of fifty thousand barrels. The brewing was done entirely with steam, and seventy-five barrels a day could be produced.

In 1863, the brewery was sold to Reese & Co. It planned to continue the manufacture of ale and porter at the brewery. P. Vidvard remained as agent. Charles B. Reese and Michael Steber were the primary members of Reese & Co. They changed the brewery name to the Mohawk Valley Steam Brewery, which produced ale and porter. By mid-1867, the brewery had been offered for sale. To purchase it, one was instructed to see F. Reese at the brewery in Ilion, P. Vidvard or D. Pier in Utica.

JAMES DYGERT BREWERY, 1868–74

In 1868, James M. Dygert purchased the Mohawk Valley Brewery in Ilion from Reese & Co., along with an adjacent malt house near Steele Creek and the Erie Canal on the west side of town. In 1869, Dygert entered into partnership with Samuel Morgan, W.C. Buchanan and S.B. Johnson to form Morgan & Co. Samuel Morgan was listed as a forwarding and commission merchant, maltster, brewer and farmer in the 1869–70 *Herkimer County Directory*. Morgan died suddenly on October 10, 1869. The other partners ran the brewery until 1874, when it ceased operation.

ILION BREWING COMPANY, 1874–87

In 1874, Sayer Spedding bought the brewery on Canal Street. The brewery had offices at 17 West Main Street. The brewery was refurbished to a capacity of 6,375 barrels per year, which was obtained. Operating the brewery at this level proved to be overly optimistic. In 1875, production dropped to 4,793 barrels. By 1877, the capacity of the brewery had been reduced to 3,000 barrels per year. At some point in time, Spedding's son, Frank, became involved in the brewery.

The brewery produced only 2,353 barrels of ale in 1879. This total had dropped to 1,236 barrels by 1881. Clearly, the brewery was in trouble. Competition from larger breweries in Utica, along with beer made in the

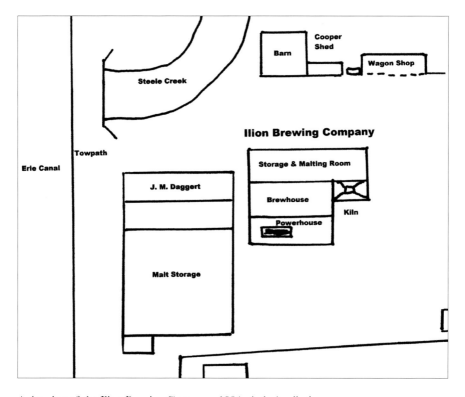

A drawing of the Ilion Brewing Company, 1884. *Author's collection.*

larger brewing cities like Rochester and Albany, was the primary reason for the decline.

Sayer Spedding had his license revoked on June 20, 1881, for selling liquor at the brewery that was consumed on the premises. Spedding had allegedly refused to let a man named Simpson play on a private billiard table at the brewery. As a consequence, Simpson turned Spedding in to the authorities. Spedding had his license reinstated a short time after. J.W. Kinne was foreman at the brewery.

The Ilion Brewing Company was formed in 1884 at 22 Canal Street to try to keep the brewery afloat. This did not work, and the brewery was closed shortly thereafter. The brewhouse was a three-and-a-half-story building with five vats on the first floor, two vats on the second floor and three vats on the third floor. There was also some storage in the attic. To the left of the brewhouse when observing from the canal was an attached two-story malt house. The malting was done on the first floor, and barley and hops were stored on the second floor. To the right of the brewhouse was an attached one-story building that was the powerhouse. It had a forty-horsepower engine. Attached to this building was a one-story coal shed. Between the Erie Canal and the brewery was a large malt house owned by James Dygert (Dagget). The property also included several detached buildings.

After the brewery was sold in 1887, Sayer Spedding worked as a brewer at the Oneida brewery until 1901. He died at his home on North Washington Street in Mohawk on August 15, 1905. The cause of his death was paralysis, and he was seventy-six years old. He was born in Yorkshire, England, in 1829 and came to America in 1871. Before coming to America, Spedding was a brewer in South Church and in Bishop Auckland, but he was declared bankrupt at age thirty-three.

MOHAWK VALLEY BREWING COMPANY, 1887–98

On July 22, 1887, the Ilion National Bank sold the brewery property to William McTierney and Christopher H. Mooney of Utica. They immediately began to renovate the buildings and equipment to be able to commence brewing as soon as possible. They changed the name of the brewery to the Mohawk Valley Brewing Company. This name had been used previously by a brewery in Little Falls, New York, but was no longer in business. C.H. Mooney was president of the new brewery and resided at 11 West Clark Street. The brewery had a stated capacity of three thousand barrels per year. McTierney sold his interest in the brewery to Mooney on February 20, 1890, for $6,500.

On May 20, 1890, Central New York experienced a very heavy rainstorm, which caused much flooding. In Ilion, water had begun overflowing the canal and Steele's Creek by noontime. The water ran in torrents down through the brewery yard and into gardens and cellars on West Clark, North and River Streets. The lower parts of the malt house and brewery were filled with muddy water, but little damage was done. The grain stored on the lower level was soaked but otherwise unharmed. After a short cleanup, work returned to normal.

When the proprietors of the brewery opened their office on June 26 of that year, they were startled to find the shattered remains of their safe strewn about the floor. Apparently, sometime between 10:00 p.m. and 5:00 a.m., the office had been entered and the safe blown up. The burglars entered the building by cutting the wire screen protecting a window and then breaking the window. Once inside, the safecrackers drilled a hole about a half inch in diameter through the top of the safe and, by means of a small tin tube, deposited sufficient gunpowder to blow both huge safe doors completely off. The safe had been used previously in the office of the *Saturday Globe* in Utica.

For their efforts, the thieves made off with some papers, a small note and about $8 in cash. They also took two revolvers and some steel punches from a desk in the office. They did not take any of the beer stamps that were in the building. It was believed that the thieves were after money ($275) the brewery had received earlier in the day. However, this money was removed to another location before closing up for the day. The police believed the job to be the work of professionals, and the thieves were never caught.

In November 1887, a worker named Higgins fell into a large vat, five feet deep, striking his head. It was thought he had a broken neck, and he remained unconscious for over two hours. His neck wasn't broken, and he eventually recovered. By 1891, C.H. Mooney had either died or moved. James H. Mooney became manager of the brewery, and he resided at the Briggs House in Ilion. Also employed by the brewery at this time were Jas. and Chris Mooney.

The brewery hadn't changed much since 1884. The brewhouse now had four vats on the first floor, two vats on the second floor and four vats on the third floor. The malt house was used for storage. The brewery was powered by steam, and the lights were run on kerosene. The adjacent malt house of Daggert was still there, and the detached building remained the same.

A delegation from the National Brewery Workers' Union, the Local Labor League and the Trades Assembly visited the brewery on March 28, 1895, to present a contract calling for a two-dollar increase in pay. The brewery readily agreed to the change and signed the contract. This was not a good decision, as brewery sales did not justify the increase. As a result, the brewery went bankrupt in early 1896. On March 15, 1896, Justice Hiscock, of the Supreme Court in Syracuse, appointed James H. Mooney and A.D. Morgan as temporary receivers for the brewery. Poor business was cited as the cause for the brewery's problems. Mooney was assigned to represent the stockholders and Morgan the creditors. The liabilities of the company were listed at $15,604.50 and the assets at $8,389.33. By May 1896, Frank S. Hoefler of Ilion had been appointed permanent receiver for the company. The brewery was officially closed sometime in 1897. The adjacent malt house was used by the West End brewery as a warehouse.

In June 1898, the idle brewery was purchased by the Mohawk Milling and Malting Company for a nominal consideration, subject to liens of $4,000.

Mohawk Valley Brewery in Ilion, New York, circa 1890s. *Author's collection.*

This marked the end of brewing in Ilion, New York. The old brewery property was deeded to the village of Ilion in 1900 for an electric light plant. This plant still stands today.

In 1904, James H. Mooney ran a café (saloon) and liquor store at 10–12 West Main Street in Ilion. He lived at 24 West Clark Street. After this, he worked at the armory, was an agent for Met. Ins. Co. and was an accountant at various times.

CHAPTER 11
LITTLE FALLS BREWERIES
1838–1904

The city of Little Falls is located twenty-three miles to the east of Utica in Herkimer County. The city lies on the slope of a narrow, rocky defile. The river that flows through the city falls forty-five feet in less than a mile, creating a number of cascades. Little Falls was first settled around 1723 due to the need to portage around the falls. The first residents were mostly German Palatines. The first settlement was destroyed by Indians and Tories in June 1782. It was not resettled until 1790 and was known as either "Rockton" or "Rock City." The village was first incorporated in 1811 and reincorporated in 1827. Little Falls was chartered as a city in 1895. The first canal constructed to bypass the falls was the Western Inland Canal in 1792, but by 1825, it had been replaced by the Erie Canal. Little Falls was a major cheese center from 1850 to 1875.

General Herkimer of Revolutionary War fame is buried on the outskirts of the city. Little Falls was the home of David Burrell, who patented the first technically sound oil burner that could burn both liquid and gaseous fuels. He also had patents on many other items. The author of the Pledge of Allegiance, Francis Bellamy, lived in Little Falls. The current population of Little Falls is 4,950.

LITTLE FALLS BREWERY, 1838–83

In 1838, William J. Beattie and his brother Jonathon came to this country from their home in Dumfrieshire, Scotland, and settled in Little Falls, New York. They constructed a brewery and malt house on the corner of Main and William Streets in Little Falls, which they named the Little Falls Brewery. The brewery had a capacity of one thousand barrels a year.

On March 20, 1858, William J. Beattie Jr. was born, and when he was old enough, he helped his father in the business. In 1874, the brewery produced 2,015 barrels of ale. Production in 1875 dropped to 1,644 barrels.

The brewery produced 912 barrels of ale and porter in 1879. By 1881, production had fallen to 669 barrels. Competition from larger breweries in Utica, Albany and Rochester caused most of the loss in sales experienced by the brewery.

In 1883, the brewery was discontinued and transformed into a hotel. William Sr. died on June 7, 1888, at the age of seventy. He was born in Scotland and came to America at the age of eighteen. His brother John died on July 26, 1893, at the age of seventy-four. William Jr. succeeded to the property, but it is not known what he did with it.

Several years after the brewery closed, on July 19, 1885, John Riley was arrested for stealing seventy-five feet of lead pipe out of the old brewery. Riley had taken this pipe at various times and sold it. One day, he made the mistake of cutting off a water pipe that still contained water. The cellar filled up with water, and this was discovered. He was arrested shortly thereafter and sentenced to six months in the Albany prison.

In early January 1895, it was announced that Joseph Schermer had made arrangements to open a sausage factory that would be located in the old brewery building on William Street. By late January, Schermer had changed his mind and decided to locate his sausage factory in the Haley Building on Second Street.

GERHARD BREWERY, 1868–78

In 1868, Nicholas Gerhard (Gearhart) started a brewery and hotel at the corner of Third and Main Streets in Little Falls. The brewery produced lager and strong beer and had a 320-barrel-a-year capacity. The brewery produced 263 barrels of ale in 1874 and 321 barrels in 1875, bringing it up to capacity. The year 1878 was the last year the brewery was in operation. Nicholas Gerhard is listed in the 1886 Little *Falls City Directory* as a carriage trimmer.

Mohawk Valley Brewery, 1886–89

In March 1886, James J. Grace, along with Michael A. Grace and T. W. Baker, formed a partnership. They leased the property known as the West Storehouse on German Street, south side, for the purpose of establishing a first-class ale brewery. These gentlemen all resided at the Grand Central Hotel. The brewery became known as the Mohawk Valley Brewery.

James J. Grace was the brewer and came from the famous establishment of the cream ale brewery of Granger & Gregg located in Hudson, New York, where he had been employed for two years. Prior to this, he had served a full apprenticeship for five years in England and Ireland and spent some time in Australia pursuing the same business.

Michael A. Grace, James's brother, was in the wholesale liquor business in New York City. Thomas W. Baker had been a traveling salesman for four years for Granger & Gregg and would perform the same service for this brewery. The brewery had a capacity of three hundred barrels per week.

The plant was established on what was known to the trade as the "tower system," which was advocated by M. Pasteur and Professor Faulkner, the two most eminent authorities on brewing. Everything employed in the business was of new construction and of the latest design. New equipment was acquired and installed. In the first brewing, some difficulty was met in reaching a satisfactory degree of perfection owing to the quality of the water.

On April 14, 1886, the brewery moved a fifty-horsepower boiler that weighed over five tons, which it had recently purchased, to its building on the south side of the river. Near Mill Street, the forward part of the wagon broke down, but repairs were made and the rest of the trip was uneventful. The brewery purchased a fine team of dapple-gray horses weighing over 2,800 pounds in May of that year. The brewery had a capacity of three hundred barrels per week at this time.

The brewery got off to a poor start. The malt that was purchased was bad, and the water used was hard. The bad malt was apparently used for about three months before it was discovered. The firm needed almost two months to determine what the problem was. Brewers from New York and Albany were called in to make examinations of the brewing process and to analyze the water. Finally, the firm purchased some malt from George Boomhall of Mohawk and tried brewing another batch. This brewing came out fine, which led to the conclusion that poor malt and water were the problems.

James Grace had purchased some six hundred bushels of malt based on a sample that he had. In hindsight, he wished that he had the grain examined by an older expert who might have spotted the problem. At first, he made no mention of the malt trouble but confined his investigation solely to the quality of the water he had to use for brewing. He experimented with several test batches until he knew how to correct the hard water problem. The test batches used malt from a different source, and the final batch came out tasting great. The problem was solved—but at some cost to the new brewery.

The production of three months was dumped into the canal at a loss of nearly $1,600. The brewery could not afford this kind of loss and went into bankruptcy on September 29, 1886. The assignee was George W. Hall, and creditors were preferred to the amount of $2,000. On October, the brewery was sold to Edward Mullen of Utica for $1,465.

On October 11, Robert F. Owens of Amsterdam purchased the brewery from Edward Mullen. James J. Grace was retained to conduct the business. At this time, the name of the brewery was changed to the Little Falls Brewery. The new brewery remained strictly an ale and porter brewery, producing Canada Malt cream ales, porter and extra pale ale.

In July 1887, Owens secured the services of George Fleming as his brewmaster. Fleming had thirty five years' experience and had been employed by the Greenway Brewing Company of Syracuse. Besides owning the brewery, Owens also owned a saloon on Church Street. On October 12, 1887, a night watchman found the rear door of the saloon open. He informed the police, Owens and the bartender, John P. Murphy. Owens opened the front door to the saloon and advanced toward the rear of the building. As his did so, he plunged into the darkness down an open trapdoor some eight to ten feet. He struck his left knee against the stairs, cutting it to the bone and painfully bruising his body and head.

The open trapdoor and the back door showed clearly that the saloon had been burglarized. It was found that about $20 worth of cigars, several bottles of liquor and $145 in cash were taken. Most of the money, which consisted of silver coin, was removed from a desk that had been pried open with an ice pick. The crooks were apprehended the following day in Tribes Hill and were committed to jail.

Owens sold his interest in the brewery in late 1887 to New York City parties. Michael A. Grace acted as their agent. The first brewing was ready for the market in January 1888. Assurances were given that a very superior quality of ale would be manufactured.

Advertisements in the 1888–89 *Little Falls City Directory* list the extra pale ale selling at six dollars a barrel and "present use" selling at five dollars a barrel. The brewery also states that half barrels were always on hand for family use, and it guaranteed its ale to be strictly pure. At this time, the brewery was listed as being on the corner of German and Jefferson Streets.

In January 1888, a number of Utica capitalists met with the idea of founding a new brewery in Little Falls. This does not appear to have amounted to anything and is not mentioned again. T.W. Baker, a former partner in the brewery, accepted a position as a traveling salesman for the Quinn & Nolan Brewery in Albany. The brewery burned down on December 25, 1888, and that was the end of this brewery. It was never rebuilt.

Michael Grace Brewery, 1897–1904

In 1897, Michael Grace returned to Little Falls and leased from William Perry the western half of a stone building located near lock thirty-seven in the city. He planned to install a modern brewery with all the best equipment for producing beer. The brewery had a five-hundred-barrel capacity and ran until 1904, when it closed for good.

CHAPTER 12
MILFORD BREWERIES
1994–PRESENT

M ilford, New York, is a small village located about eight miles south of Cooperstown in Otsego County. The village sits on Route 28 and is approximately forty-seven miles southeast of Utica, New York. The town of Milford was formed in 1796 and was called Suffrage until 1800, when it became Milford. The village was incorporated in 1890. Milford has a population of 409 people and is home to Wilbur Park, the Cooperstown Cheese Factory and the Cooperstown Brewing Company. After the Civil War, hops became the cash crop of Otesgo County, with Milford located in the center. A blight in the early 1900s wiped out the hops crop, and the local economy switched to dairy farming to survive. Today, Milford has three breweries nearby and the Cooperstown Dream Park, where teams from all over the world come to play baseball and visit the Baseball Hall of Fame in Cooperstown.

COOPERSTOWN BREWING COMPANY, 1995–PRESENT

The Cooperstown Brewing Company was formed in 1995 in the village of Milford by Stan and Brian Hall. It is located on 110 River Street in a one-story building that used to be a milk-processing plant built in the 1940s. They began brewing in the spring of 1995. The Halls installed a twenty-barrel brewing system designed by English micro-brewing pioneer Peter Austin. A brick-lined brew kettle and open fermenters were installed. In late 1995, a 120-bottle-per-

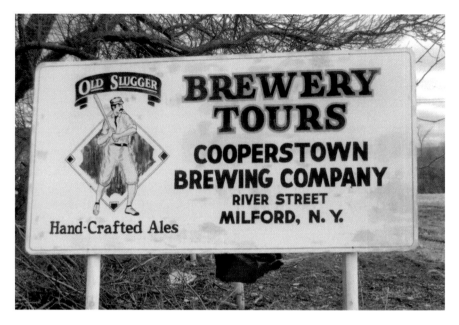

Cooperstown Brewing Company's tour sign in Milford, New York, 2014. *Author's collection.*

Cooperstown Brewing brew kettles in Milford, 2012. *Author's collection.*

Cooperstown Brewing Company's Striker beer. *Courtesy of Peter Hayes Millen.*

minute bottling line was installed. The bottling line formerly belonged to the Sam Adams brewery in Boston. The brewery produces ales, porters and stouts. It uses English barley malts, West Coast hops and English Ringwood yeast.

The names of its ales are based on baseball themes because of its proximity to Cooperstown. Its four standard brews are Nine Man Ale, Old Slugger Pale Ale, Benchwarmer Porter and Strike-Out Stout. The ales are sold in kegs and twelve-ounce bottles. The brewery also offers Back Yard IPA and Pride of Milford as specialties throughout the year. Although the beers were well received, they were somewhat hard to find, as distribution was limited.

In the fall of 2011, the brewery changed ownership. Chuck Williamson, who owns the Butternuts brewery in Garrattsville, was the buyer. The two breweries are located twelve miles apart. He believed that the breweries really complement each other. Cooperstown brews English-style ales and bottles its products. Butternuts brews American-style beers and cans its products. His goal for the Cooperstown brewery was to increase production and distribution. He immediately set about improving the recipes and brewing techniques to yield a more consistent product. Williamson thinks the beer business is a very good place to be these days. He feels that the beers he makes would have mass appeal

Old Slugger Pale Ale. *Author's collection.*

if he marketed them to areas outside the several-county area in Upstate New York where they are currently available.

Over the years, the brewery has hosted many musical and historical celebrations. Starting in 2012, the brewery sponsored a 5K run called the Brew to Brew Fun Run, which goes from the Cooperstown Brewing Company to Brewery Ommegang. The event is held in early May, and proceeds go to Habitat for Humanity.

Wes Nick joined the brewery in May 2012 as its head brewer. Since then, he has doubled production, increased efficiency and made improvements in the processing of the product. He believes that Americans love the taste of hops and has reformulated the brewery's recipes to bring out more pronounced hop flavors and aromas.

The future of the brewery looks promising. Production will be increased to address off-premises and out-of-town markets. Changing the recipes used will address the ever-changing tastes of consumers today. Tours of the brewery are available and worth checking out. While the brewery appears quite run down on the exterior, the interior is clean and well laid out. A small gift shop and taproom greet the visitor when entering the building. There are usually four or five brews available for sampling, and you can buy growlers or purchase bottles of beer to go.

CHAPTER 13
NORWICH BREWERIES

1810–1925

The city of Norwich is located forty-eight miles to the south of Utica in Chenango County. The area was first settled around 1788. The village was incorporated in 1816 and became a city in 1914. The village/city was named after Norwich, England. The city is located on U.S. Route 12 and is next to the Chenango River. It was on the Chenango Canal, which was replaced by the railroad. The current population of Norwich is 7,200.

Augustus Graham Brewery, 1810–15

On August 21, 1810, Josiah Dickenson of Norwich sold to Augustus Graham one and a half acres of land at the northwest corner of Chenango Turnpike and the road to Lewis Mills. This later became the corner of North Main and Pleasant Streets in Norwich. Graham bought the property for $150 and erected a brewery and whiskey distillery on the site. Graham was born in Scotland in April 1776. He came to the United States in 1796 and settled in Brooklyn, New York, before relocating a few years later to Norwich.

Graham obtained the rights from his neighbors to take water from any springs on their farms in exchange for a small annual fee. The springs were located to the north of the brewery. Graham stayed in the brewing business until August 20, 1815, when he sold the brewery and all the property to

A drawing of Augustus Graham from the *New York Herald*, October 1893.

Thompson Mead and Lot Clark. The brewery and distillery were purchased for $4,000.

After Graham sold the brewery, he and his brother returned to Brooklyn and started a distillery at the foot of Fisher Street, near Fulton Ferry. In 1822, he retired from the distillery and started the manufacture of white lead on Front Street. With this business, he made a modest fortune. In the summer of 1822, he conceived the idea of a free library for apprentices. With help from friends, this became a reality in the form of the Brooklyn Institute. In 1848, Graham paid off the mortgage of the institute. He died in November 29, 1851, at the age of seventy-six. After his death, he left much of his fortune to the institute as a permanent endowment.

MEAD & CLARK BREWERY, 1815–60

Mead and Clark operated the business until May 30, 1820, when Mead sold his interest in the business to Richard Crandall for $3,000. Crandall then deeded his interest in the business to Lot Clark on August 23, 1826, who now became the sole owner.

On September 24, 1827, Lot Clark sold the business to George Field. Field ran the brewery until July 12, 1835. At that time, he sold the business to Allen Mead, son of Thompson Mead, and Squire Smith. Smith sold his interest in the business to Charles Merritt sometime before 1848.

Mead and Merritt sold the brewery on June 28, 1849, to Samuel White of New Berlin and Benjamin Gardner of Edmeston for $3,000. Sometime before 1860, White became the sole owner of the brewery.

Conway & Scott Brewery, 1860–89

White sold the brewery to Cornelius Conway and Asher C. Scott on August 2, 1860, for the sum of $4,200. This new partnership lasted until July 27, 1863, when Asher Scott bought out the interest of his partner. However, later events indicate that Conway was still involved in the business until he retired in 1880. Starting in April 1869, the old brewery building was torn down to make room for a new building. By July 1870, the new structure had been completed, and the brewery was back in business. It had walls of brick on a stone foundation; it was sixty feet by eighty feet, and some portions of the brewery were two and a half stories high, comprising four or five floors. Charles Welch was employed as the brewmaster.

On Friday, December 26, 1872, disaster struck the brewery in the form of a major fire. At about 1:00 a.m., the brewery was discovered in flames. By the time the firemen arrived, the fire had spread so that all hope of saving the building was gone. The flames were first seen coming from the ventilator on the roof and soon spread to every part of the building. The kiln or drying department attached to the rear was totally destroyed. The snow on many of the adjacent buildings, including the old malt house, prevented the fire from spreading past the brewery.

The Norwich fire department had a steam engine but did not have the horses or manpower to move it through the snow. There was also a shortage of water in that location. The one hose company and the old fire engine did what they could, pumping dry the wells and cisterns in the immediate vicinity simply to retard the progress of the flames.

Conway had insurance for $20,000 on the building, equipment and stock. The stock consisted of 3,500 bushels of malt and barley, five thousand pounds of hops and a large quantity of beer. The insurance was thought to be sufficient to cover the damages. A large quantity of barrels and hogheads were kept in the storeroom and were saved due to a cement fireproof roof and walls of stone.

The loss coming at this time of year was serious, as Conway relied on previously made ale to see him through the winter. Conway stated his intent to rebuild immediately. People in the community hoped he would seek a better location for his brewery, as its present location was in a prime area for the development of the village.

By December 1873, the partners had rebuilt the brewery on the east side of the village near the river. The new brewery was called the Riverside Brewery. An ad dated December 15, 1873, announced the opening of the

Scott Brewery in Norwich, New York, after the fire, in 1873. *Author's collection.*

brewery by A.C. Scott & Son. The new brewery produced XX and XXX Cream Ales. Conway died from heart failure on September 26, 1900, at the age of seventy-one. He was born in Crulsheen, Clare County, Ireland, and came in 1848 to Norwich, where he worked at the cooper shop of Asher Scott. He was with Scott until 1852, when he caught gold fever and went to California. After a few years, he returned to Norwich and bought the Norwich Brewery with Asher Scott in 1860.

A near-fatal explosion occurred at the brewery in early December 1879, when brewer Frank Schaub was pitching the inside of a fifteen-barrel cask in the driveway west of the brewery. He was in the process of thrusting a hot iron repeatedly through the manhole of the cask to melt the pitch and spread it around the interior walls. During the last thrust, an explosion occurred similar to a cannon blast. The front of Schaub's pants were burned off, and the rest of his clothes were scorched. Asher Scott, who was standing some twelve feet from the cask, was struck by the escaping gas, and his hair and eyebrows were singed. The cask was not damaged, and nobody was seriously hurt.

The brewery prospered for many years. On September 1, 1889, Asher Scott died of cancer of the face at the age of sixty-nine. The brewery was being run by his son Thomas at the time. Asher Scott was born in Unadilla, New York, in 1820.

Thos. D. Scott Brewing Company, 1889–1900

Once Thomas Scott took over complete ownership, the brewery was renamed the Thos. D. Scott Brewing Company. He did not run it for long, as he died on July 27, 1900, at the age of forty-eight. He died at his home of acute Bright's disease. He had taken ill while on a business trip to New Berlin the week before. He was survived by his wife and two sisters but no children. As a result of his untimely death, it was decided to dispose of the brewery at auction. It was scheduled to be auctioned off on August 16, 1900.

A Thos. D. Scott Brewing Company ad, 1900. *Author's collection.*

Julius Schorn Brewery, 1900

The sale brought in a large group of people, but there were few bidders. Under the conditions of the sale, $10,000 was stated as the minimum allowable bid. A bid of $10,000 was placed, with the winning bid being $10,010. Julius A. Schorn, a well-known cigar manufacturer, had the winning bid. Schorn was elated at his bargain because he had offered a much higher sum when he tried to buy the brewery in a private sale. Schorn stated that he intended to remodel the plant, doubling its capacity, and push the manufacture and sale of Scott's Ale. However, after investing $3,000 in improvements in the brewery, Schorn determined that the venture was a financial failure.

In November 1900, Schorn opened negotiations with George W. Payne whereby Payne would purchase the brewery on December 1 for $5,000. The agreement was drawn, but the deed was not signed. The agreement provided for a forfeiture of $500 in case either party did not act in good faith. On November 30, Schorn shot himself at his home on Clinton Street at about 9:30 a.m. He was approximately thirty-five years old.

Schorn arose as usual, dressed himself and, after breakfast with his family, went down into the basement, got his gun and shot himself. The ball entered his mouth and passed out through the top of his head. His body fell onto the floor on its back. Members of the family heard the shot and rushed downstairs to see what had happened. The doctor was summoned, but Schorn was already dead.

The revolver was a new .32-caliber gun. Another revolver owned by Schorn had been hidden by his family as they were concerned about what he might do. He had been worried over financial matters for some time. The venture proved a great disappointment. Schorn had made plans to sell the brewery to ex-sheriff George Payne by December 1, but having second thoughts about the sale, he chose another way out of his difficulties. Shorn was survived by his wife, one child, a brother and two sisters. Schorn's family paid the forfeiture of $500 to Payne and then sold the brewery to John H. White of Unadilla.

NORWICH BREWING COMPANY, 1901–25

White filed articles of incorporation on October 31, 1902, in the office of the secretary of state at Albany. The capital stock was fixed at $100,000, consisting of shares of $100 each. The directors of the new corporation were John H. White, Reuben Jeffrey and Henry T. Jarrett. White renamed the brewery the Norwich Brewing Company. It was producing White's Sparkling Ale and Porter. There were still ads being placed that referred to the brewery as the Riverside Brewery.

In early 1903, the brewery was shut down to undergo necessary improvements to keep up with demand. On July 25, 1903, the improvements were completed and the brewery started back up. White invested $15,000 on the improvements, which included an electric light plant. Whitman Merritt joined the brewery as a bookkeeper. In December 1905, the brewery sold ten thousand barrels of White's Sparkling Ale to a Brooklyn customer, to be delivered in 1906.

A Norwich Brewing Company advertising fan, early 1900s. *Leo collection.*

In early March 1907, Louis Burkhard of Norwich was given a judgment for $2,544 against the Norwich Brewing Company in a contested case in which the counter claim was $5,000. Burkhard had sold the brewery casks, which the brewery claimed were not properly made. The brewery appealed the case. The case came before the court of appeals in early 1909, and the court upheld the judgment. The brewery had to pay Burkhard.

John H. White and James M. Lucas went to Buffalo in May 1907 and bought forty head of cattle, which they then brought back to Norwich. Previously, they had brought thirty acres of fine grazing land adjacent to the Riverside Brewery on the east side of the Chenango River. The plan was to use the malt and grain left over from the brewing process to feed the cattle. If successful, they felt that they could replace western beef with a local product.

In 1908, White was elected president of the Chenango County Agricultural Society. The following year (1909), he was nominated for sheriff. The article also mentioned that White was wealthy. Starting in

Ad from the *Norwich Village Directory*, 1910.

March 1909, the brewery began marketing a new product called White Ribbon. It looked like beer, tasted like beer and contained all the healthful and nutritive qualities of beer yet had no alcohol. A government license was not required to sell it, and it was absolutely non-intoxicating.

While at work at the brewery on a Saturday morning (December 23, 1912), P.J. Hill accidently scalded his right foot. The injury was so serious that he was taken home, where he was confined for several weeks. Hill was washing out a large tank with boiling water when he splashed a quantity of the water into his boot, filling it nearly to the knee. His foot was scalded by the water to such a degree that the skin came off.

A 1914 ad shows that M.A. Scott was connected with the brewery as a manufacturer. Based on other documents, it would appear that White still owned the brewery and that Scott might have been the brewmaster. The brewery was producing one hundred barrels of White's Sparkling Ale a day.

Disaster hit the brewery on August 27, 1915, when fire broke out, completely destroying the plant. The brewery and its contents were worth around $50,000. A total insurance of $30,000 was carried on all the buildings, equipment and contents.

As a crowd left the Colonia Theatre on the night of August 26, they saw a light in the direction of the brewery, which was just across from the fairgrounds. Most folks thought that some of the men at the fairgrounds had built a large fire.

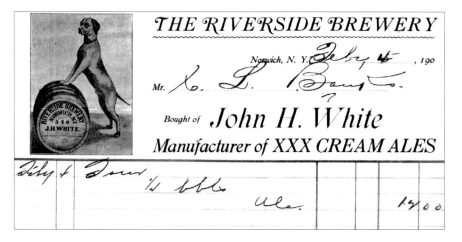

Riverside Brewery letterhead, 1904. *Author's collection.*

Norwich Brewing Company, circa 1910. *Author's collection.*

As the light grew brighter, they realized that the brewery was on fire. At 11:50 p.m., the alarm was rung. George Waters, who worked at the brewery, was awakened by people yelling about the brewery being on fire. When he looked out, he saw flames issuing from the cupola of the main structure. The fire was too far gone by the time the firemen arrived. It burned furiously for over three hours before finally being brought under control. It was impossible to get the steamer to the river's edge and to pump water from the river because of the condition of the ground. There were no fire hydrants located that far out of the village. The main building had a frontage of 350 feet and was two stories high. It was of wood construction, as were the other destroyed buildings. About one thousand barrels of ale were stored in the building.

George Waters, the night watchman, stated that he and the superintendent, John Granger, had left the building at about 6:30 p.m. that evening and, at the time, everything was in good condition. The buildings were securely locked up, and there was no evidence of fire. People who lived on that road and were returning home at about 10:30 p.m. that night also stated that the brewery was dark when they passed by.

The fire was first seen coming from the cupola, which was located directly above the malt room, and it was thought that a spontaneous combustion there caused the fire. About twenty men were employed at the brewery at the time of the fire. The question remains: why was the night watchman at home sleeping and not at the brewery? If he had been at the brewery, they might have caught the fire in time. The destruction of the brewery was too heavy a loss for White, and he never rebuilt it. At the time of the fire, the brewery was owned by a stock company. John H. White owned the majority of the stock. J.H. Throop and J.M. Lucas also owned stock.

On March 25, 1918, John H. White died of pneumonia at the age of forty-seven. The last traces of the brewing business in Norwich were being removed by September 1919. An auction sale of the real property of the Norwich Brewing Company was held, and the property was bid off by James M. Lucas for $735. Lucas was appointed receiver of the company, which was being dissolved by court order. There were several bidders on the property. Mrs. Julia Armondi of Delancey purchased the property for the purpose of opening a laundry. The Norwich Bottling Works was adjacent to this property. Around this time, the old brick and stone walls of the brewery located on North Main Street were torn down.

On July 7, 1925, an old barn that was formerly part of the Norwich Brewing Company burned to the ground while the chemical engine crew, who had no water available, watched it burn. The glare of the flames lit up the sky, and it was estimated that five hundred motorists were at the scene in the belief that there was a disastrous fire. Aside from the building, the chief loss was a new automobile owned by Dwight Eccleston, whose home on the premises was formerly used for the office in brewery days. The fire department had been called out a few weeks prior to put out a blaze in the barn. This fire was far more devastating.

CHAPTER 14
ONEONTA BREWERIES
1898–PRESENT

The city of Oneonta is located sixty-two miles to the southeast of Utica in Otsego County. The area was settled mainly by Palatine Germans and Dutch settlers who arrived around 1775. Originally, Oneonta was known as Milfordville. The name was changed to Oneonta in 1832, and the village of Oneonta was incorporated in 1848. Oneonta became a city in 1908, and its nickname is "City of the Hills." In the Iroquois language, the word *Oneonta* is believed to mean "place of open rocks." When the Delaware and Hudson Railroad reached Oneonta, the village began a growth spurt. Oneonta was once home to the largest locomotive roundhouse in the world. The current population of Oneonta is 13,900.

ONEONTA CONSUMERS' BREWING COMPANY, 1909–11

A group of gentlemen gathered in 1909 to discuss starting a brewery in Oneonta. The city did not have a brewery at the time, and the nearest operating breweries were in Utica and Binghamton. These operations were a fair distance away, and the gentlemen thought a local brewery could be a profitable concern.

They called the brewery the Oneonta Consumers' Brewing Company. They filed articles of incorporation with the secretary of state on September 20, 1909. The capital stock was set at $100,000, consisting of shares of $100 each. The directors of the brewery were Theodore Brix and Joseph Brenner of Spotswood, New Jersey, and Charles L. Martin, William Le Reum and W.A. Kelly of Oneonta.

They planned to erect a substantial building of brick and concrete along a convenient point on the Delaware & Hudson tracks. The cost of the building was estimated at $75,000, and it was the intention to begin work on the building as soon as possible, to carry out the construction work throughout the winter months and be ready for business in the spring. By November 1909, the site for the new brewery still had not been positively settled, but they announced that they would open an office for the transaction of business by December 1.

The brewery certified to the secretary of state on August 5, 1910, that half of its capital stock of $100,000 had been paid in. The certificate was signed by William E. Hubbard, George L. Bockes and William A. Kelly as directors. The plan for a new brewery was in trouble by 1910. The remaining stock had yet to be sold, and that kept the work on the brewery from occurring. The directors were hopeful of getting more public support, but in the end, this did not accomplish anything useful. The brewery was never built.

On June 6, 1912, Justice Rudd of the Supreme Court at Cooperstown granted a nonsuit in the action brought by Fannie M. Dickson against George L. Bockes, Esquire, for damages alleging fraud, the action being based on the purchase of bonds of the Oneonta brewing concern.

The suit brought against Bockes arose over Mrs. Dickson's purchase of bonds amounting to $400 of the brewing company organized in 1909. Bockes, it was alleged, recommended the bonds to induce the plaintiff to purchase. When the plaintiff's evidence was concluded, the court granted the motion of the defendant's counsel for a nonsuit. No proof that Bockes had acted in bad faith was presented.

DRYTOWN BREWERY, INC., 1994–96

One of the earliest microbreweries in Central New York was the Drytown Brewery, Inc., which was formed in February 1994. It was located at 3 Roundhouse Road in Oneonta. The brewery was in an industrial park, which was originally part of a railroad yard. Construction of the brewery began in early March 1995 and was completed by the summer.

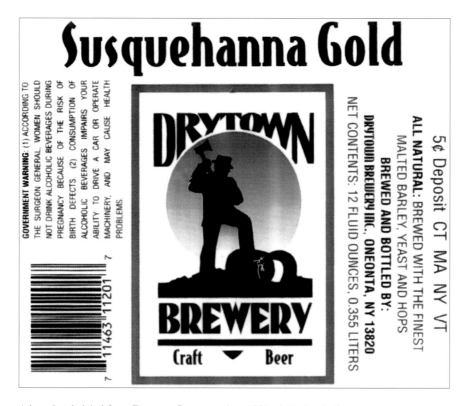

A beer bottle label from Drytown Brewery, circa 1995. *Author's collection.*

The brewery was run by Harold Leitenberger (president) and Paul Robinson (secretary and treasurer), both of whom lived in Treadwell, New York, and Michael Bishop, an agent for the brewery. Once production began, the brewery produced Susquehanna Gold, Upstate Amber Ale and First Place Ale. They produced 3,500 barrels annually, and the brews were sold in kegs and bottles. Distribution was quite limited at the time, and by mid-1996, the brewery had closed. It was probably ahead of its time, as the microbrewery craze had yet to pick up enough steam to support these small microbreweries in New York State.

In July 1996, the Drytown Brewery, Inc. was incorporated as a domestic profit corporation located in Connecticut, which is where Michael Bishop had moved. The corporation still exists on paper but does no brewing. Harold Leitenberger died on March 28, 2011, at the age of seventy-five.

ROOTS BREWING COMPANY, 2012–PRESENT

This brewery was formed in April 2012 by two home brewers, Jason Parrish and Russell Scimeca, who wanted to share their love of well-crafted beers with others. Parrish is the brewmaster and has a PhD in chemistry from Purdue University; he performed research and development at Brewery Ommegang in Cooperstown before deciding to start a brewery. Scimeca's wife, Amanda, who trained as a lab technician is apprenticing under Parrish to become assistant brewmaster. Russell Scimeca serves as the business manager of the brewery.

The brewery is located at 175 Main Street in Oneonta, New York. Scimeca and Parrish presented their plans to the city planning commission to have a restaurant that would serve homemade brew on-site. They would build a 155-gallon brewery that would produce ten barrels at a time, and they would install a kitchen to prepare food for patrons. Approval to proceed was given by the planning commission in 2013.

Much of the equipment used in the brewery has been custom designed and fabricated in central New York. A converted dairy tank is where the mash

Roots Brewing Company sign in Oneonta, New York, 2014. *Author's collection.*

Roots Brewing Company banner. *Author's collection.*

Roots Brewing Company building in Oneonta, 2014. *Author's collection.*

starts. The custom-made boiling kettle was designed to provide a rolling boil and to optimize hop utilization. The brewery employs open fermentation to allow the gases to escape quickly.

So far, its brew offerings are an American India Pale Ale, an Abbey Tripel Ale, a Blonde Ale and a Brown Beer. The alcohol by volume ranges from 5.8 percent to 8.3 percent for these offerings. They stated that they want to become an integral part of the local economy by supporting local farmers, producers and artisans.

CHAPTER 15
ORISKANY FALLS BREWERIES

1816–1901

T he village of Oriskany Falls is located twenty miles to the southwest of Utica in Oneida County. The village was first known as "Cassety Hollow" and was settled around 1794. It was incorporated in 1880, and the name was changed to Oriskany Falls after a local waterfall. The village had two known breweries. The current population is approximately 730 people.

H.M. HIND BREWERY, 1816–68

The first brewery in Oriskany Falls was built by Thomas Hind around 1816. His brewery lasted until around 1857. On April 20, 1854, L.W. Thompson committed suicide at the brewery by hanging himself. He worked at the brewery but was an alcoholic. Prior to his successful hanging, he had made an unsuccessful attempt at his home two weeks earlier.

Thomas Hind died by 1864, and his son Henry M. Hind took over the business. Henry M. Hind was born in Utica on August 17, 1833. He formed a brewery called H.M. Hind & Company in 1864, and it lasted until 1868, when it was closed. Henry M. Hind became brewmaster for the Cold Spring Brewery in Waterville. After working at Waterville for a few years, he moved to Watertown in 1873 and worked at the Haas Brewery and then at P. Munday's malt house. He died on December 26, 1883, of dropsy (today, dropsy is known as edema or the swelling of soft tissues in the body) at the age of fifty.

ORISKANY FALLS BREWING COMPANY, 1868–1901

In 1868, the Oriskany Falls brewery was built on the site of Elisha Fowler's Distillery on College Street. The buildings covered an acre of ground on Brewery Lane (now Scerbo Lane). The brewery was constructed by Perry S. Risley, who employed Henry Hind as his brewmaster. Risley's nephew Captain Eugene Smith was taken in as a partner. He erected more buildings with sides of quarry stone and wooden roofs. A malt house was built with a capacity of seven thousand barrels per year. The mash tub had a one-hundred-bushel capacity, but only fifty bushels were processed at one time. Mashing and grinding were done with the aid of a ten-horsepower engine. Malting capacity was fifteen thousand bushels. The brewery employed twelve people and bought barley grain from local farmers.

Smith purchased Risley's interest in the brewery on April 21, 1876, making him the sole owner. The brewery received a new delivery wagon built by M.H. Norton in June 1877. The wagon was a substantial platform spring

Risley and Smith's brewery from the 1868 *Oneida County Atlas of Oriskany Falls, New York*.

Oriskany Falls Brewery letterhead, 1881. *Author's collection.*

wagon using the Davis pattern. It had a top and rack and was designed expressly for delivering bottled lager.

The brewery apparently made a product that appealed to a variety of people. An article in March 1878 indicated that it was doing a good business with a temperance hotel in Brookfield. It was said that the brewery team stopped there every few weeks, and a portion of its cargo was unloaded. The brewery produced 3,758 barrels of ale in 1879 and 4,087.66 barrels of ale in 1880.

Smith's sister, Amelia, continued the business for a short time after his death. She then sold it to Herman Morgan and James A. Douglass in 1882. They formed H. Morgan & Company to run the brewery, which produced pale, amber, stock ales and porter.

Morgan claimed his product, which was made from local hops and the purest spring water, was a superior ale. The brewing capacity was ten thousand barrels per year. Fifteen people were employed at the brewery at this time. Four teams of horses and wagons were used in delivery and were constantly in use. Large quantities of the brewery's product were shipped by rail to the surrounding area.

By March 1887, Perry S. Risley and his brother Frank had gone bankrupt. Perry had originally sold the brewery to concentrate on hop growing. His brother was also a hop grower. Apparently, they had some trouble with their

H. MORGAN.   J. A. DOUGLASS.

Oriskany Falls Brewery.

H. MORGAN & CO., Proprietors.

BREWERS&MALTSTERS

PALE, AMBER AND STOCK

Ales and Porter.

ORISKANY FALLS, N. Y.

Ad from the *Waterville Times and Hop Reporter*, 1882.

crops and could not meet their obligations. In March 29, 1892, the brewery covered an acre of ground and had a capacity of seventy-five barrels a day.

Herman Morgan died at his home on Cottage Street on April 4, 1894, after a short but painful illness at the age of eighty-two. He was born on Gorton Hill, Brookfield, New York, on May 29, 1841, and moved to Oriskany Falls in January 1862. His wife died the year before.

James P. Hennessy Sr. became brewmaster in 1888 and stayed in that position until the brewery burned in 1901. In 1901, he purchased the Wells Hotel Block on Main and Madison Streets in Oriskany Falls and established Hotel Hennessy. He ran the hotel until 1926, when he turned it over to his son, Raymond. He died on August 17, 1934, at the age of sixty-nine after being confined to his house for several weeks.

After Morgan died, Douglass bought the brewery from the Morgan estate for $6,900 on December 7, 1894. He also bought from the estate a house on Main Street known as the Howe place for $1,590 and other personal property

Oriskany Falls Brewing Company letterhead, 1897. *Author's collection.*

consisting of horses and vehicles. He brought his son, C.L. Douglass, into the business and created the firm Douglass & Son. C.L. had graduated from a brewer's school in New York City with the degree of brewmaster.

At the May 6, 1898 meeting of the brewery workman's union held in Utica, the main business was to vote on withdrawing the union label from the brewery and to rate it unfair until such time as the proprietor, C.L. Douglass, complied with the rules and regulations of the union and made restitution. The members of the union claimed that reports were received by them indicating that the workmen at the brewery were not being paid. All efforts to verify this rumor were made, but without success. It was also alleged that Douglass had not paid his assessments to the union. A letter was received from Douglass stating that the brewery workmen in his plant would drop out of the local union, as the benefits they derived did not compensate them for the cost of retaining membership.

W.C. Russell accepted the position of traveling salesman for the brewery in June 1901. Dominick Jordan, a well-known farmer and hop grower, died on November 8, 1901. For many years, he had worked at the brewery as its maltster.

A fire broke out at the brewery at 11:15 p.m. on December 23, 1901, and it was totally destroyed. The fire was caused by spontaneous combustion in the grain bins. At this time, the brewery was a three-story wooden structure occupying around 120 square feet of ground. The brewery employed seven to eight men full time but had increased to around fifteen during the summer.

The fire was a hard one to fight, and the firemen were hampered by a lack of water pressure and a bursting hose in addition to the cold weather. The malt house, a stone building near the brewery, caught fire also but was saved by hard work. A house, barn and icehouse were also saved but sustained some damage. The fire was extinguished by 3:00 a.m. The total loss was estimated at $35,000, with $10,000 insurance on all the buildings. The insurance would not come close to replacing the brewery. Douglass, the head of the firm, was an elderly man and was so seriously prostrated during the progress of the fire that he was taken home and placed under the care of a physician.

Ale was the principal product of the firm, and its territory embraced all the southern tier counties. Although the brewery was very prosperous at the time of the fire, it was not rebuilt. In March 1902, an ad was placed in the local papers offering the former brewery site for sale.

On January 18, 1904, Perry S. Risley passed away due to pneumonia at the age of eighty. He was survived by two sons and a daughter and was buried in Waterville. James A. Douglass died in his home after a long illness on August 24, 1926, at the age of eighty-nine. He was born in a log home in the town of Floyd on October 23, 1837. During his life, he worked as a farmer, a teacher, a brewer, a lumber and produce businessman and in a canning factory. He helped form the Oriskany Falls fire department, which is named after him: Douglass Hose Company. He was very active in the community. In his will, he left the Village of Oriskany Falls a park that was in front of his home.

CHAPTER 16

ROME BREWERIES

1851–1936

The city of Rome is located seventeen miles to the northwest of Utica in Oneida County. The city was built astride the Great Carrying Place. The name refers to a portage road between the Mohawk River to the east and Wood Creek to the west, leading to Lake Ontario. This short portage was the only overland section of a trade route stretching over one thousand miles between Lake Ontario and the lower Hudson River. The region was the scene of bloody fighting during the French and Indian War. The British built Fort Bull in the 1750s to defend the area, but the French and their Indian allies massacred the British at the fort shortly afterward. In 1758, a large British force reclaimed the area and built Fort Stanwix. After the war, this fort was abandoned.

At the start of the Revolutionary War, American forces reoccupied and improved the fort. A British siege failed, and the fort shielded America's northwest frontier until it was abandoned in 1781. The village began to thrive with the construction of the Rome Canal in 1796. The village was called Lynchville, after a man named Lynch who originally owned the land. Rome became a city in 1870, when it was incorporated. Rome has become known as the "City of American History." Another name for Rome is the "Copper City." Revere Copper Products Incorporated was formed in Rome in 1928. Jesse Williams founded America's first cheese factory in Rome in 1851.

Between 1951 and 1991, the Rome Air Development Center was located at Griffiss Air Force Base. The base also was home to the Air Force B-52 nuclear bombers. In 1999, Woodstock 1999 was held at the former air force base. Since the closing of the former air base, it has been redeveloped for other purposes. The runways are still used as an emergency landing field for planes requiring long runways. The current population of Rome is 33,725, which is down significantly from Rome's peak, when the air force base was in use.

ROOT & BACKUS BREWERY, 1851–58

The Root & Backus brewery was located near the arsenal in Rome and the Watertown railroad depot. It became the second brewery to be set on fire in Rome in 1858. The brewery was not rebuilt after the fire.

On April 30, 1858, a fire broke out at about 3:00 a.m. at the brewery owned by J.H. Root. The brewery, along with the attached dwelling house and barn, was completely destroyed. The dwelling was occupied by a brewery employee who managed to save some of the household property. The horses in the barn were also rescued. The property was insured for $3,000, which it was felt would cover the loss.

An indolent and dispirited fellow named Sylvester Adsit for several weeks had been sleeping in the loft of the building. His remains were found burned to a crisp. There was no indication that he might have started the fire. The fire was thought to have originated in the dry kiln.

Root almost burned his own house down that same night. When the alarm was given for the fire at the brewery, Root threw the match he had used to light a lamp in his bedroom on the carpet in his haste to get to the brewery. Returning to his house after the brewery fire, he discovered so much smoke in his bedroom that he was unable to enter. Subsequent efforts, aided by others, allowed him to finally put out the fire and save his home. Root rebuilt the brewery afterward, but his partner, Backus, left the company.

ROOT & BALDWIN BREWERY, 1858–69

Root formed a new partnership with a man named Baldwin after the fire in 1858. They rebuilt the brewery on the same site. The brewery was struck by lightning on June 16, 1860. A stove pipe was fractured, a table and stove were upset and a pump burst open. Fortunately, no one was hurt. In 1869, the brewery was set on fire, becoming the second brewery that year to burn. The brewery was not rebuilt after the fire.

O'Neil's Brewery, Unknown–1869

This brewery was located near the old canal. In 1869, O'Neil's brewery was the first of six breweries in Rome to burn to the ground. All the fires were thought to be set by arsonists and happened during a four-year period. O'Neil's was not rebuilt afterward.

Martin Miller Brewery, 1857–71

Martin Miller started a brewery in 1857 in Rome on Court and Jay Streets. On August 3, 1871, a fire was discovered at the brewery in the rear part of the structure near the icehouse. This was located on the west side of the brewery. Miller's living quarters were attached to the brewery and were located on the north end. Everything was destroyed by the fire, but the family made it out safely.

While the fire was raging, a man named Caswell observed a man crawling out of a pigpen nearby. Caswell gave a description of the man to the police, and they later arrested Rudolph Glass, who fit the description. Miller's memorandum book and wallet containing thirty-two dollars were discovered on Glass, who said he had found them and was keeping them safe to give back to Miller. Mrs. Miller had kept these items in the pocket in her dress, which was found in the pigpen with the pocket torn out.

Glass was brought before the judge, where he pleaded guilty to theft and was committed to jail on $1,000 bail. He was also suspected of setting the fire at the brewery to cover his tracks. He was then linked to another recent robbery in the area. Glass had only recently moved to Rome from New York City and worked at a local mill.

Besides losing the buildings, there were sixteen barrels of beer in the tubs that were lost. There were also twenty-five barrels of beer in the cellar that were saved. Miller had insurance, which amounted to $1,400 on the buildings, $1,000 on the stock and $300 on the household furniture. The brewery was not rebuilt after this. The Miller brewery was the fifth brewery in Rome to burn.

FRANCIS GOLDSMITH BREWERY, 1857–72

Francis Goldsmith began a brewery in Rome on Liberty and Jay Streets in 1857. He was born in Bavaria, Germany, on August 9, 1829, and he arrived in this country in 1850. Henry Goldsmith bought the brewery from his brother in 1870.

A devastating fire struck the brewery on May 17, 1872. The brewery and Goldsmith's home were completely destroyed by the fire, along with several other buildings in the area. Goldsmith and his family narrowly escaped from the burning buildings in their nightclothes. A man was run over by steamer

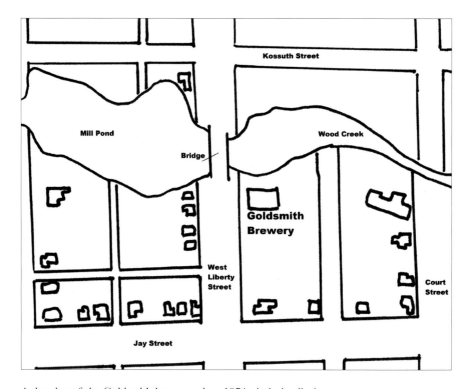

A drawing of the Goldsmith brewery, circa 1874. *Author's collection.*

No. 1 while on the way to the fire. It was believed that the fire was purposely set, as this was the fifth brewery destroyed by fire in two years in Rome. A few months earlier, Goldsmith had interrupted an attempt to burn the brewery. Several shots were fired at him at the time.

The fire was first discovered in the malt house, which was constructed of wood like all the other buildings that were burned. The fire originated in the northwest end of the building. Goldsmith had $6,000 worth of insurance on all the property, including the brewery, stock, fixtures, barns, etc. The barn was not destroyed. Losses were estimated at about $10,000. About $500 worth of hops and three to four hundred bushels of malt were totally destroyed. It was not known at the time how much of the ale stored in the cellar could be saved.

The brewery was rebuilt with the help of money from Peter Vidvard of Utica, who became the owner. In the spring of 1875, Vidvard offered the brewery for sale. He indicated that it was in condition to be run without expense for repairs.

Francis left to start a grocery business. Henry stayed as the brewmaster, and a gentleman named Christian ran the business. This setup continued until May 1877, when Vidvard closed the brewery. The brewery started back up in September 1877 under the name the Vidvard Brewery and was run by his son Julius.

The Goldsmith family relocated to Herkimer, New York, where Anna Goldsmith purchased a brewery from Peter Hellmick in 1877. Francis (brewmaster) and Henry (superintendent) worked at the brewery. Francis Goldsmith died on October 5, 1908, at St. Elizabeth's Hospital in Utica after an illness lasting for several months. He had been living in Utica for the past five years.

Oneida Central Brewery, 1858–1901

Lawrence Gaheen was born in County Wexford, Ireland, in 1831. John Kelley was born on June 30, 1830, and also lived in County Wexford, Ireland. Gaheen and Kelley were best friends and came to America in 1850. Gaheen went to Canada, and Kelley came to Rome. Kelley secured work on a farm and then became a baggage man for a railroad. Around 1853, Gaheen came to Utica and was employed by George Hammill as a farmhand. He went west for a while before returning and entering a co-partnership with Hammill in the farm and milk business. In 1858, Gaheen, along with his brother-in-law (John Kelley), formed a brewery in conjunction with Hammill. They purchased the property on Depeyster Street and the Erie Canal from Jacobs and Campbell and built their new brewery. At this time, they knew very little about the brewing industry, but they learned quickly. They hired an experienced man to run the brewery. John Amtmann was the brewer from around 1867 to 1884, when he left to become the brewer at Evans & Giehl.

The brewery burned to the ground with all its contents on January 6, 1870. The building was covered by insurance but the contents only partially. The brewery had just received a large shipment of barley malt. The origin of the fire was not known, but it was surmised that it started in one of the kilns. The brewery was immediately rebuilt with a capacity of about fifteen thousand barrels a year. The new structure was made of brick, which, while more expensive, stood a better chance of surviving a fire. The new brewery was finished by the middle of July.

On December 31, 1874, a fire broke out in Jacobs and Campbell's storehouse and was totally destroyed. The brewery was located right next to this building but was not harmed, as there was not much wind when the fire began and the firemen quickly contained it. Hammill sold his stake in the brewery to Lawrence Gaheen in 1875 and returned to farming.

In 1877, the brewery produced 3,244 barrels, making it the second-largest brewery in Rome. This dropped to 2,402 barrels in 1879. The following

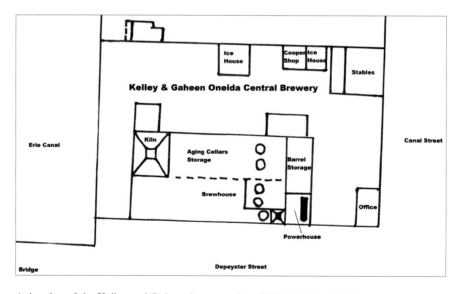

A drawing of the Kelley and Gaheen brewery, circa 1899. *Author's collection.*

year, production at the brewery had increased slightly to 2,795 barrels. It was still the second-largest brewery in Rome. On July 15, 1880, the brewery replaced its old fifteen-horsepower boiler with a thirty-two-horsepower boiler. By 1881, the brewery had regained most of the losses it sustained since 1877, increasing its output to 3,411 barrels of ale.

Burglars entered the brewery on March 19, 1882, by obtaining entrance through the adjoining cooper shop. They bored a hole through the door with a large auger and slid the bolt aside. The burglars took a few dollars in silver and a torn Canadian bill and were never captured.

Kelly and Gaheen decided to build a new brewery in 1884. They let a contract for their new brick brewery on Washington Street, opposite the Arlington Hotel, to Parry and Jones in July. The plans were prepared by architect Schillneer.

On April 8, 1888, Lawrence Gaheen died of Bright's disease at his home at the age of fifty-seven. He started to suffer with kidney difficulties about a year before his death. He continued to attend to the business until March 27, when the pain became unbearable. He became bedridden around April 5. He had three sons, one of whom was employed at the brewery, and two daughters.

After Lawrence Gaheen's death, Francis J. Gaheen (son of Lawrence Gaheen) became John Kelley's partner in the business. Like most other brewers of the time, the brewery sold brewery grains to local farmers. An ad was run in May 1896 advertising the fact.

The safe in the office of the brewery was blown open by burglars early on the morning of May 31, 1898. The office was located in a detached one-story brick building, eighteen feet by twenty feet, which stood in the southwest corner of the property. The burglary was not discovered until 4:00 a.m., when Francis

Francis Gaheen, circa 1900, from the *Rome Daily Sentinel.*

and Simon Gaheen arrived at work. Francis found the rear door standing ajar, blocked by a big chunk of soft coal. The office was a scene of wild disorder, with books and papers scattered over the floor. Francis called his brother—who was in the brewery proper, which was a separate building—and notified the police.

The burglars had first gone to a new frame house being constructed nearby and had taken two chisels and a brace. The chisels were used to break into the office. The brace was used in boring a hole in the safe door. All were afterward found on the floor. It was clear that the men were not pressed for time, for they took time to go back to the barn in the back of the brewery to get a carriage cushion, a sleigh cushion and a lap robe. The two cushions were laid on the floor in front of the safe, while the lap robe was soaked in a mud puddle and laid on top of them. A bottle was found that contained a few grains of gunpowder, and there were three little paper cornucopias through which the gunpowder had been poured into the hole. Then a fuse was attached and lit. The door was ripped from the hinges and the frame and filling thrown on the cushions. The steel sheet forming the front was hurled across the room, a distance of eighteen feet, and struck wainscoting, cracking one board the entire length and making a deep hole where the knob struck. The lock on the cash drawer in the safe had been broken by burglars about fifteen years earlier, so only papers were kept in there. Money wasn't kept in the safe, as the brewery had been robbed three to four times over the years. As far as could be told, the burglars got nothing for their efforts. The police eventually caught the criminals.

Francis J. Gaheen died on December 21, 1898, at his home from inflammation of the brain. The previous week, while walking to the brewery, he fell on an icy sidewalk, severely hitting his head. He did not think much of it until several days later, when his head became very painful. A doctor was called and prescribed bed rest, but Gaheen gradually became worse and, after several days, died. He was thirty-three years old.

The main brewery building in 1899 was two stories high and divided in two sections. The front section, which was on the street, contained a malt mill on the first floor, grain and beer storage on the second floor and storage in the basement. A small three-story section was located on the right side of this building and contained two tanks. Behind the front section were the brew kettles on the first floor, grain storage on the second floor and vats in the basement. A malt kiln was located on the left side of this section. A small two-story attached building was behind the kiln. The engine room was located in the front of the brewery on the right side of the main building and was two stories high. Behind this was an attached one-story building. In the rear of this building was another one-story building. The brewery office was a one-story building completely detached from the brewery and located on the corner. A two-story detached icehouse and a one-story detached icehouse were at the back of the property. There were several other detached buildings on the property.

In 1900, the brewery was producing filtered, cream and stock ales and porter. Its ales were very popular and in high demand. The brewery had three malting floors, and the brew kettle had a capacity of fifty barrels. Kelley retired from the brewery in 1901 due to failing health. He died on May 12, 1910, after suffering a stroke on May 8. He had been in a semiconscious state since the stroke.

S.P. Gaheen & Company, 1901–02

The Oneida Central Brewery, which had been conducted by the firm of Kelley and Gaheen, passed into the hands of a new company on July 1, 1901. The new firm was called, S.P. Gaheen & Company. The reason for the change was the retirement of John D. Kelley after running the brewery for forty-three years.

During the past year, the brewery had been repaired, and new, modern equipment was purchased and installed to greatly increase its capacity. Simon P. Gaheen was the active member of the new firm. He had worked for the old firm for fourteen years. For twelve of those years, he was the brewmaster.

Independent Brewing Company, 1902

Simon Gaheen was the principal owner, and he conceived a plan for forming a new company in 1902 to obtain partners that would supply capital to make improvements to the brewery.

The new company would have a capitalization of $50,000 divided into $50 shares. Local wholesalers and retailers of ale and lager would be the interested parties. The new name chosen for the firm was the Independent Brewing Company.

Gaheen indicated that about 6,800 barrels of lager and 13,900 barrels of ale were being consumed in Rome. All of the lager and 20 percent of the ale came from sources located outside Rome. This represented $125,000 paid out annually to foreign breweries. The old firm produced only ale and could make 50 barrels a day. The new firm would produce ale and lager. Unfortunately, Gaheen could not raise the needed funds, and the brewery was closed in late 1902.

Simon Gaheen died on August 4, 1937, after a lingering illness at the age of seventy. He was born in Rome on June 17, 1867, the son of Lawrence Gaheen. He married in 1894, and his wife died in 1914. After working at the brewery, he got a job in the annealing department of the General Cable Corporation, and before that, he worked for the Rome Brass & Copper Company. He retired in 1931.

In 1903, the brewery buildings were leased to a group that wanted to establish a knitting mill. The knitting mill was originally located in Boonville, but Rome was felt to be a better location. The name of the firm was the Mystic Star Mills. This was not successful, as in 1904, the brewery buildings were leased to Graves Bro. for its general storage and forwarding business. The old Kelley and Gaheen brewery property was offered for sale in 1907 for a very low price by the firm of Baldwin and Stone, real estate agents. The Graves Bros. still occupied the building at this time under a lease.

VIDVARD BREWERY, 1877–84

The Vidvard Brewery was located on Liberty Street and Wood Creek and was the former Goldsmith brewery. After Peter Vidvard closed the Goldsmith brewery in May 1877, his son, Julius, took over in August 1877. This was a lager beer brewery. Vidvard had a grand opening on the evening of August 9.

In January 1878, Vidvard completed construction on a mammoth icehouse measuring seventy by twenty-four feet. The inside and outside were covered in matched pine. It had zinc flooring with trenches for the water to drain. At the time, it was one of the fanciest icehouses in central New York.

In 1878, Edward Evans moved to Rome and entered into partnership with Julius Vidvard in the brewery. He bought out Vidvard in 1879. Edward Evans was born in Utica on January 1, 1849. In 1863, he moved to Brooklyn and operated a sash and blind factory for fifteen years.

Evans produced 2,150 barrels of beer in 1879. This increased to 4,050 barrels in 1880, making it the largest brewery in Rome and the fifth largest in central New York. In 1881, the brewery increased its production to 4,315 barrels.

VIDVARD & EVANS

BREWERY

Cor. Liberty st. & Wood Creek,

ROME, N. Y.

All Orders by Mail Promptly Attended to.

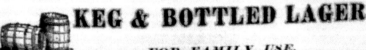

KEG & BOTTLED LAGER

FOR FAMILY USE.

Ad from the *Rome Daily Sentinel*, 1878.

Lager Beer & Ale Brewery,

EDWARD EVANS, Proprietor.

VIDVARD BREWERY,

Liberty Street, and Wood Creek,

ROME, N. Y.

The Largest Lager Beer Brewery in Central New York.

Ad from the *Rome Daily Sentinel*, 1880.

In 1884, he entered into partnership with John Giehl. Peter Vidvard, the original owner of the brewery, died on July 1, 1885, at the age of sixty-four. In early 1887, this brewery was available for rent, as the previous owners were planning on building a new brewery.

On April 3, 1890, a person by the name of Hoffsetter, who was living in the Vidvard brewery, attempted suicide by drinking a quantity of laudanum in beer because he couldn't find work. He was unsuccessful in his attempt.

In October 1896, the old brewery was leased and being remodeled into an ale brewery by the heirs of the late John Amtmann and would become the Amtmann Brewing Company.

EVANS & GIEHL BREWERY, 1884–1923

On July 9, 1887, the firm of Evans & Giehl announced that it would soon begin erecting a new brewery and malt house on West Dominick Street in Rome. All the buildings were constructed of brick with tin roofs. The brewhouse was three stories high, with a frontage on Dominick Street of sixty feet and extending back forty-one feet. The malt house was in the rear of the brewhouse and was sixty by sixty feet and three stories high. The malt kiln was twenty-six by twenty-six feet and was the last building constructed. The new brewery was completed in November and ready to brew in 1888.

Ale was to be brewed on a gravity system in which the process started on the top floor and proceeded from floor to floor until it reached the cellar,

Evans & Giehl brewery letterhead, 1899. *Author's collection.*

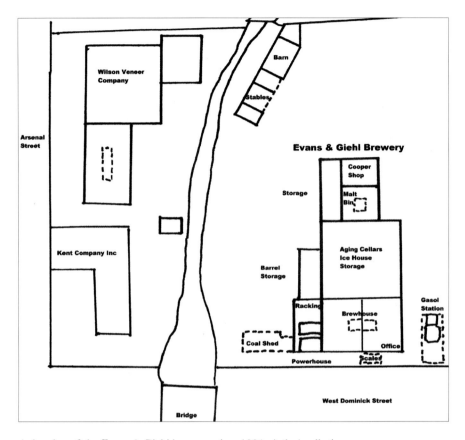

A drawing of the Evans & Giehl brewery, circa 1904. *Author's collection.*

where the ale was put into barrels. The cost of the project was $35,000. The capacity of the new brewery was 150 barrels per day.

When Evans and Giehl began their business, John Amtmann left the Kelley and Gaheen brewery to become the brewmaster at the new brewery. He remained there for five years, after which he left to partner with Captain Julius Smith in the firm of Julius Smith & Company.

On June 4, 1891, the firm demanded cash payment in full for some stock for which George Giehl had not collected, and upon his declaring his inability to pay, it had him arrested and confined in the Rome jail on a charge of misappropriation.

Bad luck did not escape employees working at this brewery. On January 26, 1892, Edward Price, who worked at the brewery, fell from the malting room through an opening to the floor below, a distance of twelve feet. He sustained a fractured collar bone on his right side and some internal injuries.

At a Brewery Workers' Union meeting held on March 4, 1900, the committee that was appointed to visit all the saloons in the area that sold Evans & Giehl beers made its report. All the saloon keepers stated that they would not sell this beer while the union continued its boycott. This boycott continued until the brewery conceded to the union's demands. In November 1900, the brewery was connected to the Rome Home Telephone Company's exchange. Its number was 232.

Burglars entered the brewery on Saturday morning, July 16, 1892. They unlocked the front office door and passed through the front office and the transom to the back office, where the safe was located. With a sledgehammer, the handle of the safe was broken off and the hole filled with gunpowder. The door was blown open, and the books and contents of the safe were strewn about the floor. The door to the safe was not blown off its hinges but was completely ruined. The cash drawer was broken open, and $7.71 was taken. A clock that had been wound up that night had stopped at 1:00 a.m., probably due to the explosion, indicating at what time the burglary took place.

Moses Murphy, the bookkeeper, balanced the books the next day, and it was shown that $7.71 was lacking to strike a balance. When the burglars left the building, they locked the door. Footprints on the outside indicated that two people were involved. It was believed that they thought that since it was Saturday, it would be the payday for the brewery, and thus there would be a large sum of money in the safe. They left no clues for police and were probably professional thieves.

The threat was then made that unless Giehl paid the money owed, he would be sent to state prison for three years. Giehl had no money, but his wife did. The brewery obtained from her the money, which she paid believing the payment necessary to release her husband from jail. The Giehls, who were German in birth, claimed that the brewery took advantage of their unfamiliarity with American law to extort money from them. In May 1893, the case was brought to court, and in the end, it was decided in favor of Evans & Giehl.

Evans died of dropsy (called edema today) at his home (420 West Dominick Street) on March 22, 1897, at the age of forty-eight. Later, the brewery was operated by Mr. Fitzgerald until it closed on the advent of Prohibition.

In 1899, facing the brewery from the street, you would see a three-story brick building. On the right-hand side, there was an office on the first floor, coolers on the second floor, hop storage on the third floor and storage in the basement. The left side of the building had the engine room on the first floor, malt mill on the second floor and mash tub on the third floor. A one-story wash house was attached to the left of the main building. Behind the main brewery was a two-story malt house, and behind this was a three-story malt kiln. To the left of the malt house and behind the wash house was a one-story attached barrel house. A detached one-story shed was near the barrelhouse, and several detached one- and two-story buildings were near the stream. There was a one-story icehouse located in the back of the property. Power and heat were provided by coal-fired steam generators. City water was available, and light was provided by candles.

Emil Hoffstetter, a fireman at the brewery, was arrested on April 10, 1901, on a charge of assault in the second degree alleged to have been committed against John Niedle, a shoemaker. Apparently, Hoffstetter and Niedle had an argument at the brewery on April 9. Hoffstetter struck Niedle in the face with a coal shovel. The only witness to the argument was a tramp brewer named Frank Lutz, whom Niedle took to the brewery in the hope of getting him a job. Hoffstetter furnished bail and was released. Niedle was in the hospital with numerous bruises about his face and head. Brewery officials say that Niedle had no right to go into the engine room. He ignored a sign that said, "No Admittance" and therefore had no business there. The hearing was adjourned until April 21. At that meeting, the case was referred to the grand jury, which convened on May 8. Hoffstetter was found guilty of second-degree assault and given a fine. On August 30, 1914, Hoffstetter committed suicide in Camden, New York. He went into a barn and shot himself twice, once through the mouth and the second time through the heart.

In 1903, the brewery signed the pay levels of the Coopers' International Union, Local No. 192. It provided for a workday of nine hours, eight hours on Saturday; fifty cents per hour for overtime; and wages of eighteen dollars per week.

Several changes had been made to the brewery buildings by 1904. The detached shed and icehouse were gone, and two one-story buildings were added to two sides of the malt kiln. A small one-story building was added near the engine room, along with a coal bin. The brewery had two ice machines now located in the main building. The ice machines had capacities of twenty tons and seven tons. Light was now powered by gas and electricity.

In mid-June 1906, the brewery hired a drilling firm to find an abundant supply of pure water for use in the manufacture of its beer. In early July, it struck a pure spring at over one hundred feet below the surface with a temperature of forty-eight degrees.

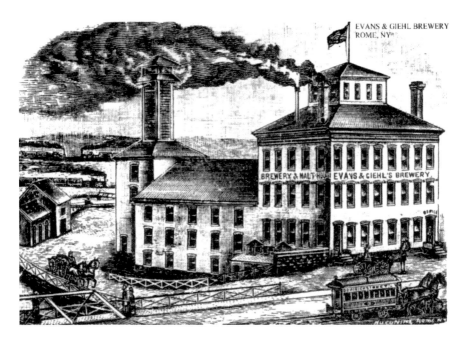

A drawing of the Evans & Giehl brewery, circa 1915. *Author's collection.*

An Evans & Giehl Brewery metal sign. *Rome Historical Society collection.*

An Evans & Giehl Brewery beer tray, circa 1905. *Smith collection.*

The brewery was robbed on January 11, 1907, but little was taken. The robbery was discovered by Moses Murphy, bookkeeper for the brewery, when he entered the building in the morning. He noticed that the knob of the office door was broken off, and the cash drawer in the office had been pried open. All the drawer contained was some small change and a few cigars. The other drawers were opened and ransacked but contained nothing of value. The safe was not tampered with. Three men were caught by January 21 with much of the loot still on them. They had also robbed a couple meat markets and admitted to going through the brewery on two different occasions. They were convicted after confessing and sent to jail.

An advertising fan for Evans & Giehl Brewery, circa 1910. *Author's collection.*

The remaining building of the Evans & Giehl Brewery, 2013. *Author's collection.*

On May 25, 1915, Louis Mertz discovered a fire in the cupola of the three-story brewery building and turned in the alarm. The blaze was quickly put out, but water running through the building did considerable damage to stocks of grain, hops and malt. The estimated loss was $10,000 and was covered by insurance.

After Prohibition was repealed, the brewery was refurbished and became the Rome Brewery, Inc. in 1934.

Julius Smith Brewery, 1859–96

Julius Smith was born in Neulasheim, Baden, Germany, on November 20, 1824. In 1847, when the Baden army joined the German revolutionaries, he was compelled to flee the country. He went to Switzerland and then came to America in 1849. He arrived in Rome in the later part of 1849 and opened a hotel in a house that stood where the Owens, Williams, & Co.'s planning mill was located on South James Street. He also worked as a carpenter and became quite wealthy. In 1854, he organized the first military company in Rome and thereafter was known as Captain Julius Smith.

In 1857, he bought the wooden brewery of John Miller on Wood Creek in Rome between Van Patten's sawmill and the arsenal. Under Smith's management, the business grew to a point that the building occupied all the space between Liberty and Court Streets.

On April 27, 1871, at about 5:00 a.m., a fire was discovered at the Julius Smith brewery. When first discovered, the barn that was on the south side of the lot and the brewery building just north of it were engulfed in flames. The family house, which was quite a bit farther north of the brewery, was also discovered to be on fire. The family was wakened by Jacob Tice, the night watchman in the business part of the city. The family barely managed to get out of their house with a few possessions before the structure was fully enveloped. While the firemen were unable to save Smith's brewery, they were successful in keeping the fire away from Goldschmidt's brewery, which was located nearby.

The fire was thought to be suspicious, as no fire had been in the brewery for the past two days for brewing purposes. Two men were seen in the vicinity about an hour before the flames were discovered. Losses were as follows: on the buildings (malt house and brewery) from $12,000 to $15,000, insured for $8,000; and household goods, from $1,500 to $2,000, insured for $800.

There were one thousand bushels of barley in the building and around five hundred barrels of beer. The horses and cows were saved, but four pigs and numerous poultry were killed. Smith planned on erecting a new brewery building during the summer.

The brewery produced 421 barrels of beer in 1879. The following year, production dropped to 335 barrels of beer, making it the smallest of the Rome breweries. The year 1881 saw production drop to 327 barrels.

In 1886, after Smith suffered a severe stroke, he found two partners to help him run the business—John Amtmann and Theodore Widman. The new partnership operated under the name Julius Smith & Company. During this time, many improvements were made to the brewery. In January 1888, the brewery started full operation and began manufacturing ales and porter. The washing, boiling and fermenting rooms; the malt house; and cellars were put in good condition. New machinery was added, including a steam pump.

On May 13, 1891, Thomas Murphy, who drove a wagon for the brewery, had an accident. While rolling a barrel of beer from the wagon to the platform at the freight house, the plank slipped, and he fell on the edge of the barrel, knocking out several teeth. Moving around very heavy barrels of beer could be hazardous, especially for Thomas. He seemed to be accident prone. On September 14, 1891, he was kicked on his right leg just below the knee by one of the horses hitched to his wagon. The bone was broken, and he had to be attended by a doctor. This put him out of work for quite awhile.

In 1893, the brewery employed seven people, who were paid $4,200 a year in wages. The company brewed about 4,500 barrels of beer a year. The brewery was struck by lightning on June 24, 1894. A hole was torn in the roof, and a chimney was partially demolished.

Theodore Widman sold his interest in the brewery in July 1895 to his two partners: Julius Smith and John Amtmann. He had been with the company

Julius Smith brewery letterhead, circa 1890s. *Author's collection.*

during its eight years of existence but wanted to pursue other options. Prior to his time at the Julius Smith brewery, he had worked for the brewing firm of Evans and Giehl as a bookkeeper.

Captain Julius Smith died at his home (509 West Court Street) on January 6, 1898, of paralysis complicated by neuralgia. He was seventy-four years old. In 1886, he suffered a severe stroke of paralysis. This was followed by a second stroke in 1896 from which he never recovered.

Philippina Smith Brewery, 1897–98

After John Amtmann's death in 1896, Julius Smith's wife, Philippina, took control of the brewery. Julius Smith was incapable of running the day-to-day operations of the brewery. He still provided guidance and advice to his wife. The brewery became known as the Philippina Smith brewery. The brewery consisted of a large two-story building that was broken into three sections. The southern section contained the malt kiln, the middle section contained the brew kettle and the northern section contained an office and storage. Attached to the brewery on the pond side of the building was a one-story icehouse. To the south of the brewery, there was a one-story shed and a two-story dwelling. The brewery operated under Philippina's control until 1898, when Julius died. After her husband's death, she shut down the brewery

P. Amtmann & Company, 1896–1901

The heirs of John Amtmann leased the Vidvard brewery on West Liberty Street in October 1896. They planned to remodel it into an ale brewery to be known as the Amtmann Brewing Company. C.R. Heller was in charge of general management, and William J. Amtmann was the superintendent. Heller was married to John Amtmann's daughter. William Amtmann was John Amtmann's son.

John Amtmann, who had died in September 1896, was very involved in brewing in Rome throughout his life. He first worked at Kelly and Gaheen as a brewer and then at Evans and Giehl as head brewer for five years, and finally he formed a co-partnership with Captain Julius Smith under the firm name Julius Smith & Company. His career influenced his children, who began their own brewery when he died.

Driving a beer wagon could be hazardous to one's health. John Mahoney, a driver for Amtmann & Company's brewery, narrowly escaped being killed when the horses spooked and ran away. On Tuesday morning, January 19, 1897, as he was driving across the Central tracks, his team became frightened and started to run up James Street. In his effort to stop the horses, one of the bits broke. The wagon, which was loaded with several kegs of beer, struck a milk wagon parked in front of the blacksmith's shop and dragged that wagon and horse to East Front Street, a distance of one hundred feet, where the team ran into a telephone pole.

The end of the wagon pole was driven into the telephone pole, breaking both. The horses were thrown, and Mahoney was tossed down between the horses and hit the sidewalk. He cut his scalp in two places and was rendered unconscious. He was rescued by witnesses and treated by a doctor, then released. The milk wagon was totally destroyed, but all the horses came through in good shape.

A little over a year later, on Friday, March 18, 1898, Mahoney and John Hatcliff, who were driving the same team of horses, had another accident. Mahoney was in the Italian boardinghouse. Hatcliff attempted to turn the team around, but he turned too short and was thrown from the wagon. One of the wheels passed over his leg, bruising it badly. The pole of the wagon struck a tree, which stopped the team but broke the pole.

In November 1900, the brewery was connected to the Rome Home Telephone Company's exchange. Its telephone number was 235.

During 1901, the brewery added new equipment, which made it one of the best equipped in central New York. Some of the equipment was a Deckebach Patent Carbonic Gas Liquid Beer Cooler, a Torchiani's Ideal Patent Counter Pressure Racking Apparatus, a Loew's Improved Patent Beer Filter and a six-ton ice and refrigerating machine. With the addition of this equipment, the process for brewing was much improved. After leaving the brew kettle, the wort passed over a bandelot cooler into the fermenting room, where fermentation was completed. It was then put into large storage casks, where it was kept at a temperature of thirty-four degrees to mature, after which it was ready to be put into various packages. From the storage casks, it entered the Deckebach Cooler, where the beer was brought down to a temperature of thirty degrees, which liquefied the carbonic gas and kept it in the beer. From here, it went to the Torchiani Racking Apparatus, which filled the kegs. The carbonation was kept in the beer while filling by Patent Bung Locks.

The brewery signed a contract with the Coopers' International Union, Local No. 192, in April 1903. It provided for a workday of nine hours, with eight hours on Saturday. Wages were $318 per week, with fifty cents per hour for overtime.

Amtmann Brewing Company, 1902–08

In 1902, the Amtmann Brewing Company was formed by Philomena Amtmann. It was located at 514 West Liberty Street in Rome. The brewery was located to the south of the Julius Smith brewery. In 1904, the brewery consisted of a two-story building with an office on the first floor and storage on the second floor. To the north of this building was a two-story brewhouse. On the first floor were fermenting tanks and a washroom. The second floor was the mill room. The building also had storage cellars. The engine was located in the north end of this building. Attached to this building on the north side was a one-story coal shed. A large two-story icehouse was located to the south of the brewery. The fuel used by the brewery was coal. Stoves were used for heat, and steam was used to power the equipment. Light was provided by candles.

On April 24, 1906, a fire was discovered in the roof of the lean-to in the rear of the brewery, where coal was kept. Upon arrival, the fire department quickly put out the fire before much damage was done. The blaze was thought to have originated from sparks from the smokestack.

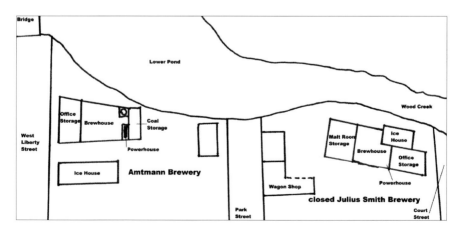

A drawing of the Amtmann and Smith breweries, circa 1904. *Author's collection.*

Everybody Calls For

Amtmann's

Patent Process

ALE.

WHY DON'T YOU?

Ad from the *Rome Daily Sentinel*, July 1902.

Philomena Amtmann put the brewery up for sale in 1910 to satisfy her creditors. A public auction was scheduled for May 25, 1910. All the brewery fixtures, machinery, engines, boilers, hogheads, tubs, ice machine and coils, barrels, piping, horses, wagons, sleighs, et cetera, were available for purchase. John B. Schwarz was the assignee for the sale. The brewery property was sold to George Gifford and F.L. Roth for $1,625.

On December 5, 1910, the assignee for the brewery made his final report to the county judge in charge of the case. Total claims against the brewery amounted to $2,700, plus a mortgage for $3,000. The assets that were sold, including machinery and real estate, amounted to $5,433. The money left over after paying the bills was divided among the creditors.

Philomena Amtmann died suddenly on October 8, 1916, after suffering a stroke at age seventy-seven. She was born in Bavaria, Germany, on May 4, 1839, and moved to America at the age of four with her parents. She married John Amtmann when she was seventeen.

Over the following years, the brewery buildings remained largely vacant; however, during Prohibition, bootleggers set up a complete distillery in the brewery vaults. On June 20, 1927, federal agents discovered the operation directly under the cobblestone driveway that ran between an old barn and the Ammon apartment house. Peter Ammon stated that he had sold the brewery property to Adam Beach of Albany.

The agents found four two-hundred-gallon stills, an eight-foot column, a condenser and three large wooden vats with a capacity of ten thousand gallons. The stills were heated by two two-plate gas burners under each still for a total of sixteen burners. Gas was furnished by a one-inch hose connecting onto a one-inch pipe that ran through the wall into the apartment house. A complete water and drainage system was found.

Employees of the Northern New York Utilities were investigating the gas pipeline supplying the apartment house, as more gas was being used than could be accounted for from the few families that lived there. After much searching, they found that the pipeline had been tapped into just before the meter. This pipe ran through an old vent hole into the old brewery vault.

The agents entered the old cellars but found they were in total darkness. One of the agents was sent downtown to procure some flashlights. The other

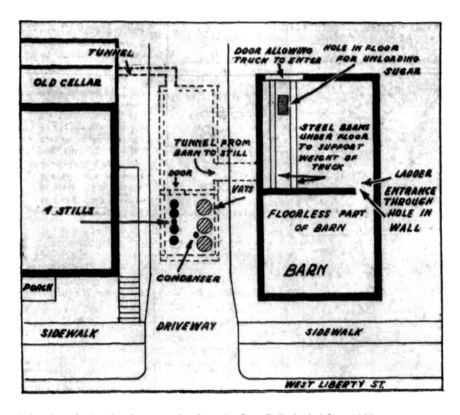

A drawing of a bootlegging operation from the *Rome Daily Sentinel*, June 1927.

agent waited in a side tunnel found in the rear of the aging cellar. This agent heard a car drive over the cobblestones directly over his head. He thought it was the other agent returning but glimpsed a pair of legs climbing down a ladder from the floor of the house into the rear house cellar. The person heard the agent moving in the side tunnel and beat a hasty retreat back up the ladder. By the time the agent followed him, the person had already taken off in his car. When the other agent came back, they started to explore the old vaults. The main vault was located directly under the cobblestone driveway. The alcohol that was found was of the corn sugar variety. The three vats were found full. The equipment looked to be fairly new and had not been used for very long.

At the rear of the unused section of the vault, a hole had been made in the rear wall, and a small tunnel was dug that turned to the left and led into the rear cellar of the house. The tunnel opened with a trapdoor into the floor of the rear cellar of the house. This part of the house was part of the old brewery and was currently being used as a garage and milk plant.

To supply the operation, a truck was driven into the barn, and the supplies were dropped through a hole into the cellars below. The finished product was also loaded into the truck through this hole. The agents drained the mash and destroyed the equipment, selling the metal to a scrap dealer. The wooden vats were left in place.

The neighbors were completely unaware of the distilling plant. After the still was found, the place became packed with spectators, many of whom went into the vault to see what remained of the operation. The operators of the illegal distillery were never caught.

ROME CEREAL BEVERAGE COMPANY, 1926

This company was located in the old Evans & Giehl brewery at 527 West Dominick Street in Rome. On March 19, 1926, five federal dry agents seized the plant of the Rome Cereal Beverage Company. They arrested the driver of a truck loaded with beer as he was about to leave the plant to make deliveries. Samples of the beverage were taken, and a large amount of stock was destroyed. The charge was possessing and transporting beer. The plant was valued at $250,000. Orders to padlock the brewery were issued in federal court on May 9, 1926. The proprietor and three employees had pleaded guilty and were given the option of jail sentences or paying fines.

Thomas Jones, the proprietor, was sentenced to one year in jail or a fine of $2,500. The three employees were given six-month sentences or $1,000 fines each. All the men chose to pay the fine. The court ordered the destruction of fifteen thousand gallons of beer and machinery. A confiscated truck, twenty-five bags of sugar and other material were sold. The company was just a front for a bootlegging group. There was no further activity of any kind until just before the end of Prohibition.

Rome Brewery, Inc., 1934–35

Late in 1932, a large force of men were engaged in preparing the old Evans & Giehl brewery for operation in the event that Congress should modify the Volstead Act to permit the manufacture and sale of beer. The property was purchased in April 1933 by Francis J. O'Brien.

Officials said that the resumption of operations would give employment to more than fifty men, all of whom would receive high wages. In addition, a number of trucks would have to be acquired for distribution of the product and drivers employed. One of FDR's 1932 presidential campaign promises was the repeal of the Volstead Act. He felt that this would help get the economy going again and employee many people. The bootlegger business would be destroyed, and crime would be lessened. Once elected, FDR's first order of business was getting the Volstead Act repealed.

Articles of incorporation were filed with the secretary of state in May 1933 by the Rome Brewery, Inc. of Rome. Capital consisted of 450 shares of common stock. Directors for the firm were Francis J. O'Brien, who had ten shares; Terrance Bush, who had five shares; and Timothy O'Shea, who had three shares.

On July 17, 1933, Francis J. O'Brien, president and general manager of the brewery, announced that his firm had received its permit from the United States Treasury Department to manufacture 3.2 percent beer. He also stated that the company had immediately applied to the State Alcoholic Beverage Control Board for its state license. The license was received on August 5.

In 1935, Timothy O'Shea was the company president. Because of the strained situation, the company said its creditors would file involuntary bankruptcy proceedings against it. The brewery was granted its petition for reorganization under Section 77B of the Bankruptcy Law on May 3, 1935, by federal judge Frank Cooper. The company could continue temporarily

ROME BREWERY, Inc. N⁰ 4574
ROME, N. Y.

4-9 193 4

_____ Received of Rome Brewery, Inc.

_____ Bbls. 1 2 Ale at $ 7 5 0 Per Bbl.

To remain the property of said firm until paid for.
Barrels to be returned in good order, on demand, or paid for.

Delivered by _____

Empties Returned _____ Bbls.

" _____ Half Bbls.

" _____ Quarter Bbls.   Permit No._____

A Rome Brewery, Inc. receipt, 1934. *Author's collection.*

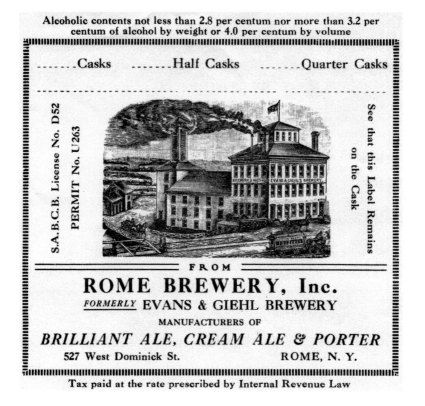

Alcoholic contents not less than 2.8 per centum nor more than 3.2 per
centum of alcohol by weight or 4.0 per centum by volume

------ Casks   ------ Half Casks   ------ Quarter Casks

S.A.B.C.B. License No. D52

PERMIT No. U263

See that this Label Remains
on the Cask

FROM

ROME BREWERY, Inc.
FORMERLY EVANS & GIEHL BREWERY
MANUFACTURERS OF
BRILLIANT ALE, CREAM ALE & PORTER
527 West Dominick St.   ROME, N. Y.

Tax paid at the rate prescribed by Internal Revenue Law

A Rome Brewery, Inc. keg label from 1934. *Author's collection.*

A Rome Brewery beer tray, circa 1935. *Author's collection.*

to operate its business until a hearing on June 2 in which creditors would be required to show cause for why the arrangement should not continue. This order stopped the impending sale of the property, which would have taken place on May 4. A June 1935 financial statement showed $53,468 in liabilities, not counting capital stock, and assets of $92,102, including plant and equipment, which represented $52,294 of the total.

The brewery shut down production in July 1935. A financial statement was filed by the brewery in federal court on October 16, 1935, that stated it had liabilities of $91,873. The court appointed a referee to liquidate the company.

FORT STANWIX BREWING COMPANY, INC.,1936-42

NOW

READY FOR DELIVERY

Fort Stanwix

ALE

Rome's Own Draught Beer

Brewed from Only the Choicest Ingredients by the Latest Brewing Science

Clubs, Hotels, Tap Rooms, Etc.

PHONE 1110

and leave your order

FORT STANWIX BREWING CO.

INC.

Albert E. Ellinger, Pres.

527-601 W. Dominick St.

Phone 1110

Ad from the *Rome Daily Sentinel*, January 1937.

On January 21, 1936, A.E. Ellinger announced that the Fort Stanwix Brewing Company had taken possession of the property of the Rome Brewery, Inc. at 527 West Dominick Street in Rome. Ellinger formed the new company in late 1935 to succeed the Rome Brewery, Inc. The Rome Brewery, Inc. had been idle since July 1935.

Ellinger stated that operations at the brewery would be started after the brewery had been subjected to thorough repairs and complete renovations. Much of the old equipment was discarded and new equipment installed. New mash kettles and new containers were set up, the floors were replaced in the cooler and in the office and the cellar was rebuilt with concrete and steel in the refrigerating room. The brewery employed fifteen men. The Fort Stanwix Brewing Company planned to turn out ale and lager under the trade name Fort Stanwix. Bernard Becker was the brewmaster.

On Saturday, November 7, 1936, an air compressor tank exploded at the brewery, injuring Becker severely. He suffered compound fractures to both legs below the knees, severe lacerations of the scalp and shock. He was taken to Rome Hospital. Becker had been testing airlines in the cellar and apparently was making changes on the condenser when the tank exploded. Becker was alone in the cellar when the tank exploded, but there were other employees in the brewery.

The explosion sent chunks of the metal tank flying to all parts of the cellar. Becker, who was standing near the tank, received the worst of it. Fellow workers found Becker lying on the floor stunned and bleeding, but he was conscious and remained so. An examination of the wreckage revealed that the explosion occurred near the bottom of the tank.

Becker died from his injuries on November 10. He was born in Pettenfeld, Prussia, on October 12, 1882. He came to the United States in 1909 and settled in Rochester, where he was employed as a brewmaster. He married in 1912 and moved to Rome in 1916. He was fifty-four at the time of his death.

Ad from the *Rome Daily Sentinel*, May 1937.

On January 28, 1937, the brewery began delivery of its Fort Stanwix Ale to local establishments. Theodore Wollensen was the new brewmaster. His father was the brewmaster for Lang Breweries in Buffalo, New York, and he had learned his trade from his father and from touring many breweries in Europe. The brewery ceased operating by the end of the year due to poor sales and a lack of money.

E. Erwin Owen became the general manager of the brewery in 1938, after he sold his insurance company. He ran the brewery until it went defunct. He died on June 22, 1948, at the age of sixty after a long illness.

Ad from the *Rome Daily Sentinel*, May 1938.

The brewery was declared bankrupt on June 20, 1940, by federal judge Frank Cooper. Ellinger was sued by Louis Link of Rome, who had lent the brewery $7,000 since September 1937 in exchange for seventy shares in the brewery. Link claimed he never received his stock until May 22, 1939, and it was defunct at that time. Ellinger claimed that he used the first $5,000 to pay the debt for the brewery buildings. Ellinger then received a $20,000 mortgage from the corporation, which he assigned to the Rome Trust Company. The judge found in favor of Link and ruled that he was entitled to $7,000 plus interest from September 1937.

The company was declared bankrupt on December 17, 1941, under Chapter X of the Bankruptcy Act. The final financial report showed that the brewery had $1,227 in cash against a debt of $95,772. F.J. De La Fleur of Utica was chosen as a referee and was assigned to liquidate the company. In 1941, the property was purchased by Kowalski and Firsenberg of Utica. They, in turn, decided to sell the property the following year.

A History of Brewing in the Heart of the Empire State

An auction was held on May 26, 1942, to sell the brewery buildings and all the equipment. The auctioneer first offered the four-story brick building and land for sale, which were subject to a $6,500 mortgage. There were no bids on them. Most of the equipment was sold for scrap value, with brass, copper piping and valves bringing in good money due to war shortages. Later that year, Morton Kowalsky purchased the buildings.

In October 1943, Max Lobenhofer entered into negotiations to purchase the brewery buildings to open a frozen food locker plant in Rome. It was called the Flavor Seal Packing Co. Locker Plant. This plant would offer complete food preparation, fast freezing and frozen storage service for meats, fish, poultry, fruits and vegetables to local people. This endeavor lasted for a couple years before going bankrupt. The building was then sold to Antonio Rodriguez, who operated a garage in the building. The building was again sold in February 1946, this time to Edward Herthum and Henry Patterson, who opened an automobile salesroom and garage that sold Chrysler and Plymouth cars.

CHAPTER 17

WATERVILLE BREWERIES
1864–1894

T he village of Waterville is located fifteen miles to the south of Utica in Oneida County. The area was settled by European Americans around 1792 and was first known as "The Huddle." The name was changed to Waterville in 1808. Hops were introduced into the area around 1820. By 1875, Waterville was known as the "Hops Capital of the World." With the introduction of rail service in 1867, Waterville became a major shipping point for hops. By the early 1900s, several years of bad crop yields (blight) had made the growers look to other sources to make money. Most turned to dairy farming. A notorious group of horse thieves, the Loomis Gang, operated in the area during the mid-nineteenth century. George Eastman (1854–1932) lived in Waterville and was the founder of Eastman Kodak. The current population of the village is 1,583.

COLD SPRING BREWERY, 1864–94

The Cold Spring Brewery was formed in late 1864, when a group of investors, headed by Edward S. Peck, formed the E.S. Peck & Company. The other partners were John Yale and George Hubbard. These gentlemen felt that a brewery was needed in the area, and with the raw materials so close at hand, the brewery would be able to succeed. Waterville was once known as the Hops Capital of the United States, and grain was abundant on the nearby farms. They purchased the old distillery owned by Amos Osborn. Osborn had built the distillery in 1802 just below the gristmill on the town line on Mill Street. It had been unused for some time, and workers began renovating the building to convert it into a brewery. The company planned to produce stock and ready-use ale. It secured the services of an experienced brewer from New York City and, by February 1865, was ready to start brewing. Demand quickly exceeded what the brewery could supply. Its capacity was forty barrels per day. Ale in half casks and for family use could be obtained at the brewery at any time. The company expanded the brewery the following year. The property belonged to Peck. The brewhouse and cooper shop were located on one side of the street, with storage buildings located on the other side. Ale and porter were produced.

A fire of unknown origin broke out in the barns at the brewery in July 1867. The two barns were completely destroyed. Two mules were killed, and two wagons with several sets of harnesses were lost as well. There was no insurance to cover the loss.

In 1869, Henry M. Hind was the brewmaster at the brewery. He had previously run his own brewery in Oriskany Falls from 1864 to 1869 but could not make a go of it. In 1873, Hind left the brewery to work at one in Watertown. He died of dropsy on December 30, 1883, at the age of fifty. After Hind left the brewery, the quality of the product decreased, and the brewery fell into financial trouble.

Peck bought out his partners in 1871 and conducted the brewery by himself for a while. Unfortunately, he could not pay all his debts, and the brewery was foreclosed and put up for sale.

The brewery was sold at a sheriff's sale in 1876 to Perry H. Smith, T.A. Smith and A.P. Smith for $3,230. Peck was retained to run the business for these gentlemen. In March 1877, Peck hired Jacob Reiber, a first-class lager beer brewer from Syracuse. The brewery was taking a new direction by producing lager beer instead of ale.

Peck was very excited about this new direction. He believed a lager could be brewed in Waterville that was as good as elsewhere in the United States. No sooner was the beer produced and placed on draught than orders far exceeded expectations. Peck's lager was a success. The brewery sold 643 barrels of ale in 1879 and 994 barrels in 1880. To accommodate the demand, plans were made to start bottling the lager. This would allow the brewery to fill orders from one to a dozen bottles to a barrel, thus covering demand from businesses to home use.

Peck left the brewery in 1881 to open up a saloon and restaurant in the basement of a building on the corner of Main and Mill Streets. A man named Reuben Tower owned the property by 1885. He was born in Waterville on January 17, 1829, and died in September 1899. Tower made his fortune as a cattle dealer and also had some of the finest horses in the county. He was active in politics and never married. Tower ran the brewery until 1894 with the help of Peck.

CHAPTER 18
WESTMORELAND BREWERIES

1868–1884

W estmoreland is located to the west of Utica in Oneida County. The village was originally called Hampton. The town was first settled in 1748 by James Dean, a missionary among the members of the Oneida

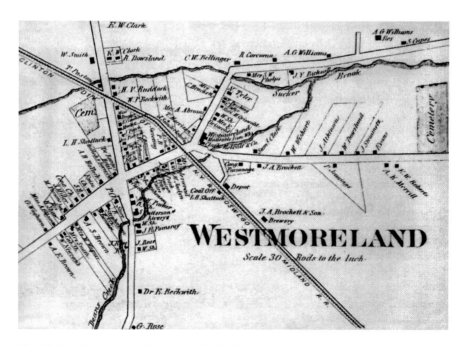

The J.A. Brockett brewery from the 1868 *Oneida County Atlas of Westmoreland, New York.*

Indian tribe. Only one brewery, which was very small, is known to have operated in this town.

J.A. BROCKETT BREWERY, 1868–84

In 1868, J.A. Brockett started a brewery in the village of Westmoreland. The brewery, called J.A. Brockett & Sons, was located near the tracks of the Rome and Clinton division of the New York & Oswego Midland Railroad near the railroad depot.

After the death of J.A. Brockett in 1877, his son A.J. took over control of the brewery. The brewery was never very big and was located in a one-story wooden-framed building throughout its existence.

The brewery sold 439 barrels of ale in 1879, 438 barrels in 1880 and 364 barrels in 1881, making it one of the smallest in the area. In 1884, the brewery closed its doors for good.

BIBLIOGRAPHY

BOOKS

Annese, Sarah, and Giancarlo Annese. *Beer Lover's New York.* Guilford, CT: Morris Book Publishing, LLC, 2014.

Bellinger, R. Edward. *Roots in the Hollow, Life in the Falls.* Brookfield, NY: Worden Press, 1989.

Bryson, Lew. *New York Breweries.* 2nd ed. Revised and updated by Don Cazentre. Mechanicsburg, PA: Stackpole Books, 2014.

Siebel, Dr. J.E. *One Hundred Years of Brewing.* Supplement to *The Western Brewer.* Chicago: H.S. Rich, 1903. Reprint, New York: Arno Press, 1974.

CITY DIRECTORIES

Boyd's Business Directory
Boyd's Rome Directory
Herkimer County Directory
Kimball's Oneida County Directory
Little Falls City Directory
Oneida County Directory

NEWSPAPERS

Amsterdam Evening Recorder, 1884–1974.
Binghamton Press, 1904–69.
Brookfield Courier, 1876–1977.
Cooperstown, The Glimmerglass, 1909–37.

Bibliography

Cooperstown Otsego Farmer, 1885–1962.
Little Falls Evening Times, 1886–1960.
Little Falls Journal Courier, 1869–1924.
Richfield Springs Mercury, 1867–1977.
Rome Daily Sentinel, 1842–1920.
Rome Semi Weekly Citizen, 1840–1903.
Syracuse Daily Courier, 1856–98.
Syracuse Daily Journal, 1853–82.
Syracuse Evening Telegram, 1898–1922.
Syracuse Post Standard, 1900–21.
Utica Daily Observer, 1861–82.
Utica Daily Press, 1882–1987.
Utica Daily Union, 1895–97.
Utica Herald Dispatch, 1899–1921.
Utica Morning Herald, 1860–97.
Utica Morning Telegram, 1919–22.
Utica Observer Dispatch, 1925–2013.
Utica Saturday Globe, 1899–1919.
Utica Sentinel, 1825–27.
Utica Sunday Journal, 1894–1902.
Utica Sunday Tribune, 1880–1910.
Utica Weekly Herald, 1863–97.
Waterville Times and Hop Reporter, 1855–2007.

Internet Sources

Beer Me. www.beerme.com.
Brew Central. www.brewcentralny.com.
Brewery Ommegang. www.ommegang.com.
Butternuts Beer and Ale Brewery. www.butternutsbeerandale.com.
Cazenovia Beverage Trail. www.cazenoviabeveragetrail.com.
Cazenovia Republican. www.cazenoviarepublican.com.
CNY Central. www.cnycentral.com.
Cooperstown Brewing Company. www.cooperstownbrewing.com.
Council Rock Brewery. www.councilrockbrewery.com.
Daily Star. www.thedailystar.com.
Empire Farmstead Brewery, Inc. www.empirebrew.com.
Erie Canal Brewing Company. www.eriecanalbrewingcompany.com.
Good Nature Brewing Co. www.goodnaturebrewing.com.
Henneberg Brewing Company. www.hennebergbrewing.com.
Register Star. www.registerstar.com.
Roots Brewing. www.rootsbrewingcompany.com.
Times Journal Online. www.timesjournalonline.com.
Tryinski, Tom. "Old Fulton, New York Post Cards." www.fultonhistory.com.
Utica OD. www.uticaod.com.

INDEX

INDEX

Index

ABOUT THE AUTHOR

In college, Dan started collecting beer cans, which he used as piggy banks to store excess pennies. In his junior year (1972), he saw an article in a national magazine about a club that was formed for people who wanted to collect beer cans. He was amazed that other people collected beer cans. He joined the BCCA (Beer Can Collectors of America), and over the next forty-one years, he collected over thirty thousand different beer cans from over fifty different countries. Over those years, he also picked up other items dealing with various local breweries like bottles, signs, trays, tap knobs, et cetera. From this, he became interested in local brewery history. Dan is a member of the BCCA (Breweriana Collectibles Club of America), the ECBA (Eastern Coast Breweriana Association), the ABA (American Breweriana Association) and the Herkimer County Historical Society.

After college, he started working at Remington Arms Co., Inc. as an industrial engineer until 2009, when he decided it was time to retire. In the early 1990s, he became interested in writing a history book about local Utica breweries. After many years of research, his first book, *Utica Beer*, came out in February 2014. During the research, he found lots of information on other breweries not located in Utica. He decided to write a second book on breweries that are within a fifty-mile radius of Utica.

Exploring the history of brewing in New York State is fascinating. Many interesting stories can be found. Dan plans to continue his research and to write more books in the future.